Child Abuse and Social Work Practice

Child Abuse and Social Work Practice

Samina Karim

LM

Learning Matters
A Sage Publishing Company

1 Oliver's Yard
55 City Road
London EC1Y 1SP

2455 Teller Road
Thousand Oaks
California 91320

10th Floor, Emaar Capital Tower 2
MG Road, Sikanderpur, Sector 26
Gurugram, Haryana – 122002
India

8 Marina View Suite 43-053
Asia Square Tower 1
Singapore 018960

Senior publisher: Susannah Trefgarne
Assistant editor: Sahar Jamfar
Senior project editor: Chris Marke
Marketing manager: Ruslana Khatagova
Cover design: Bhairvi Vyas
Typeset by: C&M Digitals (P) Ltd, Chennai, India
Printed and bound by CPI Group (UK) Ltd, Croydon, CR0 4YY

MIX
Paper | Supporting responsible forestry
FSC® C013604
www.fsc.org

Library of Congress Control Number: 2025945828

British Library Cataloguing in Publication Data

A catalogue record for this book is available from the British Library

ISBN 978-1-5296-8298-4
ISBN 978-1-5296-8297-7 (pbk)

Contents

About the author

Dr Samina Karim is an Associate Professor of Social Work and a UKRI Future Leaders Fellow, with experience of teaching social work at undergraduate and postgraduate levels in the UK and overseas. Dr Karim is an international expert in the field of child protection and is currently leading on transforming social work education in Pakistan with UNICEF. Her research interests are in the areas of child abuse and child protection and the subject of power within social work theory and practice.

Acknowledgements

With my deepest gratitude to the All-Knowing, whose guidance illuminates the path of understanding.

Dedication

In loving memory of my father, Fazal Karim, and my mother, whose unwavering love, support, and sacrifices continue to guide my efforts and intentions.

Series editor's preface

Power is a complex phenomenon much debated in academic circles, frequently discussed in political discourse and something which drives both popular and official campaigns for change. Many decades ago, when I was training to be a social worker, the debate focused on power as either a quantity that certain people or groups had or whether it was something that everyone shared to an extent and that it represented a transactional function between people in particular contexts. This cerebral debate perhaps did little directly to change the lives of people who experienced the ability of others to set the terms on which life was lived, the arguments about what was right and proper behaviour and the actions of those who assumed the right to behave in certain ways. Children and young people are often those who are 'done to', and have little say in what this means. They also have little visibility or recognition that they ought to have a voice. Social work can and should negotiate this imbalance. However, it must also be recognised that social work as an arm of the state has great power itself in the lives of people, and we must remain aware of the potential to use this for harm as well as good. As student social workers your enthusiasm and concern for best ethical practice will, no doubt, be at the forefront of your learning. Samina Karim's book will help you to keep it there as you move into novel, uncertain and difficult situations.

The UK's social and political system is ever-changing but there remain some 'touchstones' that offer a degree of stability and our recent overtures to our former partner countries in the European Union embed a concern for citizen and human rights which, again, underpins much of our value base in social work. The political situation is, however, in flux and the rise of populist politics often plays into the hands of those wishing to demonise people who are identified as different or dangerous. Sometimes a moral panic takes hold in which children and young people are considered to be out of control, feral, in need of 'tough love' or, more likely, harsh discipline. Supporting the rights and needs of children and families in vulnerable and distressed or distressing situations is the legitimate preserve of social work and understanding the ways in which these complex conditions develop and are maintained can assist you in helping those involved to negotiate a positive pathway through them.

Family and community issues, alongside the broader climate crisis and an entrenched military and somewhat existential and moral threats resulting from the wars in Ukraine and Gaza, affect us all. However, these crises exact a greater toll on some people rather than others, such as those experiencing poverty, disadvantage and marginalisation in our societies. These situations have a greater impact on children and young people than others. This heralds the importance of social work for citizen's rights and working within existing legislation whilst campaigning to change and improve the laws that seek to address such issues. It is into this febrile context that you find yourselves as social work students and to which you have the potential to offer so much. In terms of understanding these complex affairs, the practical knowledge provided within Samina Karim's book will give you some of the central tools for doing so, making this book so important to your learning for practice.

Values and ethics lie at the heart of social work practice, and so figure highly within social work education, and we address these throughout all the books in the series. The positions that we take in terms of values and ethics are, to an extent, determined by context, time and experience and these are expressed in different ways by students coming into social work education today. For those of you considering working in the area of children and families, your values will guide, enervate and drive your practice, and it will be important to reflect continually on your own experiences as a child and young person and what you bring from that to your social work role.

Since the turn of the twenty-first century, we have witnessed shifts and challenges as the marketised neoliberal landscape of politics, economy and social life may attract little comment or contest from some. We have observed the political machinery directing much of statutory social work towards a focus on individuals apart from their environment. However, we have also seen a new turn to the social in the #MeToo campaign where unquestioned entitlement to women's bodies and psychology is exposed and resisted. We have seen defiance of those perpetuating social injustices that see long-term migrants alongside today's migrants abused and shunned by society, institutions as well as individuals. Questioning the status quo in social and public policy assumed greater significance during the COVID-19 pandemic in which damage to health and social care wrought by over 10 years of austerity measures were clearly exposed. We stand at a time in which political changes seem more concerned with appearing harsher and tougher than the opposition, whatever party is in power. We also see change in extending voting rights to 16 and 17 year olds throughout the UK, giving young people a chance to effect changes at a wider level. Social policy and the well-being of others are priorities, and the work of social workers is a key service for potential and positive change.

It is likely that, as a student of social work, you will lay bare and face many previously unquestioned assumptions, which can be very perplexing and uncover needs for learning, support and understanding. This series of books acts as an aid as you make these steps. Each book stands in a long and international tradition of social work that promotes social justice and human rights, introducing you to the importance of sometimes new and difficult concepts, and inculcating the importance of close questioning of yourself as you make your journey towards becoming part of that tradition. It encourages you also to consider your own position and experiences, the fields you inhabit, the systems of which you are part and the values that guide you. This book will help you understand yourself and those with whom you work within the varied social contexts in which people live.

The importance of high-quality social work education remains if we are adequately to address the complexities of modern life whether those be of individual children and young people, families, groups or communities. We should continually strive for excellence in education as this allows us to focus clearly on what knowledge it is useful to engage with when learning to be a social worker. Questioning everything, especially from a position of knowledge is central to being a social worker.

The books in this series respond to the agendas driven by changes brought about by professional bodies, governments and disciplinary reviews. They aim to build on and offer introductory texts based on up-to-date knowledge and to help communicate this in an accessible way, so preparing the ground for future study and for encouraging good practice as you develop your social work career. Each book is written by someone passionate about social work and social services and aims to instil that passion in others. Samina Karim writes passionately and with deep knowledge that will assist you in your journey in supporting children and their families and their communities to effect positive change and to claim the futures they so richly deserve.

Professor Jonathan Parker
September 2025

Introduction

Power. Such a powerful phenomenon with such powerful consequences. Yet even though we recognise its significance throughout the human experience, we do not always seem to understand it. We may be alerted to its presence during certain experiences, but it is not something we usually reflect on with the depth it demands. Why? Because it seems complicated, controversial, or even uncomfortable? To confront power is to confront the structures that shape our lives: our systems, our relationships and even our sense of self. But power does not disappear when ignored; it continues to affect everyone and everything. Too often in the world, things happen that should not be happening, and things do not happen that should. Yet we often find it difficult to trace these events back to the choices and behaviours of people. Power is not some distant, impersonal force; it is embedded in human actions, decisions and omissions. And unless we learn to see it clearly, to name it, challenge it and reimagine it, we remain responsible for any negative impact. This is because power does not need to have negative consequences. It can be harnessed to protect, empower and to create positive change. This book is about recognising that potential and understanding how power can be used ethically and intentionally in the service of others.

Recognising how power operates is essential to understanding the realities faced by those who are most vulnerable, and perhaps nowhere is this more evident than in the lives of children. As Nelson Mandela once said, 'There can be no keener revelation of a society's soul than the way in which it treats its children', yet child abuse remains one of the most urgent and complex challenges facing social workers today. This book is written for social work students, practitioners and educators who are committed to addressing child abuse. Positioned within the Transforming Social Work Practice series, the text bridges theory and practice, offering an in-depth yet accessible exploration of child abuse through the lens of power. At the heart of this approach is a recognition that social workers must not only identify and respond to abuse, but also navigate the power relations that shape practice between professionals and the children and adults who have been affected by it.

Book structure

The book is structured across nine chapters, each aligned with the capabilities of the Professional Capabilities Framework (PCF) and informed by relevant legislation, policy and research. Beginning with an exploration of the global challenge of child abuse (Chapter 1) and the UK's policy context (Chapter 2), the text moves on to examine different forms of abuse (Chapter 3) and their wide-ranging impacts (Chapter 4). The complex dynamics surrounding perpetrators of abuse are discussed in Chapter 5, challenging common stereotypes and encouraging critical reflection.

Chapters 6 and 7 form the core of the book's distinctive contribution, introducing and developing the principles of power-informed practice (PIP) and its practice model. This framework aims to support social workers to understand and navigate the use of power in everyday practice in ethical, reflective and effective ways. The final two chapters (8 and 9) apply the practice model and its principles to direct work with children and adults affected by abuse, highlighting how a power-aware approach can lead to empowerment through social work interventions.

Professional development and reflective practice

Throughout the book, readers are encouraged to critically engage with key debates, reflect on their own use of power, and consider how broader systems influence both the prevalence of abuse and the ways in which it is addressed. Case studies, reflective questions and practical guidance aim to bridge the gap between theory and practice, with the aim of equipping social workers with the knowledge and skills needed to support children and adults in power-informed ways.

1

The global challenge of child abuse

Introduction

Child abuse is a global challenge and therefore requires an understanding of the wider landscape of concern and efforts to protect children internationally. Within the UK context, having an understanding of the global challenge of child abuse may well inform and enhance local child protection strategies. The international perspective offers an opportunity to recognise how cross-cultural dynamics may impact children within the UK. It also allows for the UK's child protection policies to be contextualised in line with the nations' commitments to international treaties and obligations. Recognising the global context of child abuse is critical, as it provides a view on the systemic factors that contribute to the abuse of children worldwide, highlighting the interconnected nature of social, economic and cultural factors that influence the success and failure of child protection efforts.

The chapter begins by exploring how cultural and economic factors intersect with the issue of child abuse globally, as well as considering how overlapping identities can increase vulnerabilities. The chapter also discusses the significance of international frameworks in responding to child abuse as a global concern. Key examples include the

United Nations Convention on the Rights of the Child (UNCRC) and the Sustainable Development Goals (SDGs). Ultimately, the global outlook reflected in this chapter emphasises the importance of collective action, as child abuse transcends borders and therefore remains a shared international responsibility.

Culture and child abuse as a global concern

To understand the complexity of child abuse on a global scale, we must first examine the various cultural contexts in which it occurs. Cultural norms and values significantly shape the prevalence and forms of child abuse, making it a complex global issue. 'Culture' refers to the shared beliefs, values and practices of a group or community of people. Culture influences how people make sense of the world and interact with others. This includes making sense of practices related to children and child-rearing. Culture therefore influences our perceptions around appropriate behaviour towards children and the acceptability of various practices. For example, in some cultures, strict discipline is seen as essential to healthy child development, while in other cultures a more permissive approach may exist. In such approaches, similarities as well as differences exist across the world. These practices are often rooted within historical, religious or social beliefs, with each nation being on its own trajectory of understanding what is or is not to be considered appropriate behaviour towards children.

Case study 1.1

Culture and corporal punishment

Families are embedded within cultural and social frameworks and thus parenting styles and child-rearing practices are recognised to be influenced by the culture or cultural capital which is inherently present in any given society (Xu et al., 2000). Therefore, an understanding of the cultural context may help predict whether certain behaviours towards children are considered to be acceptable and what the impact is likely to be on any given child. A synthesis of a wide body of research on corporal punishment has shown that its impact on children is shaped by the social and cultural context in which it occurs. Children's emotional responses often vary depending on whether their cultural environment considers such practices acceptable. Consequently, a child's perception of corporal punishment as something normal, or even beneficial, is closely linked to prevailing cultural attitudes.

When corporal punishment is widely accepted and expected within a community, parents may feel justified in using physical discipline. Simultaneously, children may perceive such punishment as a normal part of their upbringing and therefore not be affected as one may expect. In such cultural contexts, corporal punishment tends to reflect a deliberate disciplinary strategy rather than an emotional reaction to children's behaviour. This use of corporal punishment as a means of enforcing rules, rather than expressing anger, may lead to fewer negative outcomes compared to when it arises from an emotional response (Gershoff, 2002). However, such findings should be approached with caution, as most instances of child physical abuse are recognised as occurring in the context of punishment (Durrant and Ensom, 2012).

In certain countries, customary or traditional laws may override national child protection legislation, leading to inadequate safeguards for children. For example, in Australia, there is concern that customary law has been misinterpreted to justify violence against Aboriginal women and children, highlighting the need for corrective measures (Maxwell, 2016). Similarly, in South Africa, corporal punishment is widely accepted, with its widespread use often perceived as a means of protecting children from greater harm (Sloth-Nielsen, 2008). Research indicates that both parents and children in South Africa often view corporal punishment as a routine disciplinary practice in homes and schools, reflecting deeply rooted cultural beliefs (Dawes et al., 2005; Martin and Mbambo, 2011). Consequently, despite the ban on physical punishment in South African schools, one in five children continue to experience corporal punishment in educational settings (UNICEF South Africa, 2011).

Within cultures where practices such as corporal punishment are normalised, addressing abuse can become particularly challenging. On the one hand, international frameworks such as the UNCRC (1989) advocate for children's right to protection from violence (Article 19); on the other hand, in some cultures, harsh discipline is considered normal and acceptable. This cultural acceptance can contribute to higher rates of abuse and lower reporting, as such treatment is often deemed acceptable (Gershoff, 2002). Furthermore, cultural attitudes may influence the effectiveness of legal frameworks and child protection systems. Professionals working with families from diverse cultural backgrounds may become overly intrusive in their interventions or may fail to take necessary action. These outcomes can stem from misunderstandings or misinterpretations of cultural norms and behaviours. It is therefore essential that professionals balance cultural sensitivity with their duty to protect children effectively (Akilapa and Simkiss, 2012).

Focus on power

Adult–child relationships are deeply shaped by underlying social norms. These norms define the perceived rights of adults over children and can reinforce unequal power dynamics. Such power dynamics can create an environment where violence against children by adults becomes possible. Cultural constructions of authority and discipline may not only enable such violence, but also justify it, contributing to its normalisation within families and communities (Dawes et al., 2005).

Poverty and child abuse as a global concern

Global economic conditions and poverty also play a significant role in the prevalence and prevention of child abuse, demonstrating the interconnected nature of economic conditions and child welfare. Poverty and economic strain can impact children's wellbeing in multiple ways, including through heightened parental stress (Conger et al., 2000) and the increased risk of child labour and exploitation (Munir and Umer, 2023). When families are unable to meet their basic needs, their focus often shifts to survival, which can negatively impact children's wellbeing as parents struggle with the pressures of poverty.

Historically, socioeconomic factors have often been overlooked as contributors to child abuse and neglect. However, there has been an increasing recognition of poverty as a predictor of child maltreatment (Kim and Drake, 2023), with children from economically unstable families facing three to nine times more abuse or neglect compared to those from financially stable families (Conrad-Hiebner and Byram, 2020). Advancing this discussion is the acknowledgement that, even within a single country, greater income inequality across regions correlates with higher reported rates of child maltreatment, regardless of the average family income. Consequently, the most harmful environments for children are those marked by severe poverty alongside high income inequality (Eckenrode et al., 2014), aligning with findings from the World Health Organization (WHO, 2022), which identify economic stress as a major global risk factor for child maltreatment.

Research on the relationship between poverty and violence against children in the US shows that, although abuse occurs across all income levels, severe cases are more prevalent in low-income households. Social and demographic factors, such as youth and single parenthood, further increase the risk of poverty contributing to abusive behaviours towards children (Gelles, 1992). Research in the UK also reinforces the evidence on the link between poverty and child abuse, emphasising the need for children's social care to address the basic material needs of families more effectively as a key component of child protection efforts. This is because child protection systems and services often fail to adequately address the influence of low income, lack of employment and poor housing conditions on children (Bywaters and Skinner, 2022). Structural factors contributing to high poverty rates include economic policies and framework, and institutionalised ethnic and gender discrimination (Beeghley, 1988).

Economic conditions can also force children into labour and exploitative situations to supplement family income. The International Labour Organization's (ILO) Convention No. 182 on the worst forms of child labour (1999) emphasises the need for countries to address work environments that expose children to physical, emotional, or sexual abuse. However, in spite of this, millions of children are engaged in hazardous work, often as a direct consequence of poverty. Estimates suggest that 160 million children, including 63 million girls and 97 million boys, were engaged in child labour at the beginning of 2020, nearly half of whom were in hazardous work that directly endangered their health, safety and development (ILO, 2020). Such concerns are more visible in the developing parts of the world, where poverty may increase the likelihood of children entering into the workforce. In Sub-Saharan Africa, for example, there are now more children engaged in child labour than in the rest of the world combined; however, 'most children who work do so because their families depend on their wages, production or domestic work to make ends meet' (ibid., p. 61). While poverty remains a fundamental driver of child labour, evidence indicates that factors such as market inefficiencies, global supply chains, household and parental characteristics, macroeconomic and political conditions at both national and international levels and the lack of enforcement of laws and policies all play a role in decision-making around sending a child to work (Hoque, 2021).

It is important to remember however, that poverty does not necessarily lead to abuse. Poverty is often understood to be a precursor to neglect, and social workers need to avoid adopting such stereotypical perspectives, as most families who live in poverty do not neglect their children. Research evidence suggests that, despite the apparent connections between poverty and neglect, some of this may be attributed to the over-surveillance of low-income families, as well as the influence of social norms and systemic racism (Child Welfare Information Gateway, 2023), as well as parental mental health issues and domestic abuse, which collectively contribute to the phenomenon (Bywaters and Skinner, 2022). Therefore, poverty is not an isolated factor contributing to child abuse, despite service planning and delivery often adopting a 'one size fits all' approach (ibid.). Understanding the complexities present in the economic underpinnings of child abuse is therefore crucial for developing comprehensive strategies to protect children and support families in need globally.

Activity 1.1: Impact of poverty

Scenario

Layna is a single mother of two and lives in a low-income neighbourhood. Layna has two part-time jobs to make ends meet, but this leaves her with limited time and energy to supervise or spend time with her children. Her eldest son Marco is nearly 16 and has taken on part-time work at a local market to help support the family, which is beginning to interfere with his education. Her daughter Elsa is ten and is beginning to show signs of emotional distress. Despite her best intentions, the constant stress and lack of support make it difficult for Layna to provide a nurturing environment for her children.

Reflect on how economic strain can affect child welfare (both immediate and long-term implications) and consider how you would approach the following concerns as a social worker.

Parenting

a. Layna's part-time jobs do not provide sufficient income to meet the family's basic needs.
b. Due to her work schedule, Layna has limited time to supervise her children.

Child labour

a. Marco works at the market, which may expose him to exploitation and uncertain working conditions.
b. Marco's part-time work interferes with his education.

Structural determinants

a. The family lives in a low-income neighbourhood with limited community resources.
b. The local authority has little to offer in terms of support and resources for low-income families.

Intersectionality and child abuse

The term 'intersectionality' refers to the complex and cumulative way in which multiple social identities intersect and impact on individuals' experiences of oppression and privilege (Crenshaw, 1989, 1991). In the UK (as is the case elsewhere), social identities are constructed through age, race, class, gender, disability status, ethnicity, sexual orientation, nationality, migration status and religious beliefs – and remain significant indicators of inequality (Nadan and Korbin, 2018). Traditionally, these inequalities have been considered independently; however, the concept of intersectionality emphasises understanding how these inequalities exist simultaneously and interact with each other (Christoffersen, 2021). Intersectionality, therefore, challenges traditional, one-dimensional perspectives on the prevalence of social issues by recognising that individuals possess multiple, overlapping identities that influence their experiences and access to resources (Crenshaw, 1989, 1991).

When examining child abuse through the lens of intersectionality, it is important to recognise how overlapping identities contribute to varying degrees of vulnerability and risk. For example, a child from a minoritised ethnic background who also has a disability may be more vulnerable to abuse than a child who does not experience the same structural disadvantages. Economic factors also influence the nature and prevalence of abuse, and it is reasonable to assume that a child from a minoritised community may also face systemic inequalities such as poverty or limited access to resources and support. Access to power, often overlooked, is also a crucial and highly impactful component of social structure that significantly influences child vulnerability (Nadan and Korbin, 2018). Therefore, understanding these intersecting factors is essential for developing effective strategies to protect children and support those at greater risk.

Activity 1.2: Intersectionality and power

Access to power is not evenly distributed across society. Children's experiences are shaped by the social structures around them. Systemic inequalities such as racism, poverty, ableism and gender discrimination, can restrict access to power and resources, increasing levels of vulnerability. Effective child protection must go beyond a 'one size fits all' approach and respond to the diverse, intersecting identities that influence each child's lived experience. Recognising and addressing these disparities is essential for creating inclusive and effective child protection strategies.

Reflective questions

1. *Self-reflection*: What are your intersecting identities (e.g., race, gender, class, ability, religion)? Have you ever felt disempowered or excluded because of one or more aspects of your identity? What impact did that have on you?
2. *Understanding vulnerability*: Think of a child who belongs to more than one marginalised group. How might these intersecting identities increase the risk of abuse?
3. *Policy in practice*: How can child protection policies be designed to better account for intersectionality and unequal access to power? What changes would you recommend?

The development of international child protection frameworks

In recognition of the global challenge of child abuse, the international community has developed a number of frameworks aimed at promoting the safety, rights and wellbeing of children. These frameworks reflect a growing understanding that effective child protection requires coordinated international action, rooted in shared principles of human rights and social justice. Over time, key instruments have shaped international child protection systems and influenced how governments, organisations and professionals respond to abuse. This section briefly traces the development of these international frameworks, highlighting their origins, evolution and impact on child protection practices across the world.

The Geneva Declaration and the UN Declaration of the Rights of the Child

The *Geneva Declaration of the Rights of the Child* (League of Nations, 1924) was the first formal international document to recognise the unique needs of children and the responsibilities of adults towards them. Adopted by the League of Nations, it laid the groundwork for modern global child protection initiatives. The Declaration outlined five key principles, emphasising children's rights. These foundational ideas were later expanded within the 1959 UN Declaration, which introduced ten principles that continue to influence child rights policy today (UNICEF, n.d.b):

1. Every child without exception is entitled to the rights outlined in the Declaration.
2. Every child is entitled to special protection through the law and other means which enables their development physically, mentally, morally, spiritually and socially. In the enactment of such laws, the best interests of the child shall be the paramount consideration.
3. Every child has the right to a name and nationality at birth.
4. Every child is entitled to social security, and has the right to sufficient nutrition, housing, recreation and healthcare, including pre and postnatal care.
5. Children with disabilities are entitled to special education and care.
6. Children are entitled to grow up in loving home environments and can only be separated from their mother in exceptional circumstances. Society and public authorities have a responsibility to care for children without families and those without adequate means of support.
7. Children are entitled to free and compulsory education, at least in the elementary stages. The best interests of the child will be the guiding principle of those responsible for providing education and guidance.
8. In all circumstances children should be the first to receive protection and aid.
9. Children have the right to be protected from all forms of neglect, cruelty and exploitation and should not engage in work before an appropriate age, or in any circumstances where working conditions would impact on their development.
10. A child has the right to be raised with values of understanding, tolerance and friendship towards all people in the world.

(UNGA, 1959)

Activity 1.3: From international to national principles

While reviewing the principles outlined in the UN Declaration (1959), you may notice that some of the language is familiar. This is due to the shared principles that underpin child protection across the UK. Through an online search, see if you can find where the following two statements are used within UK child protection policies and guidance:

- the best interests of the child
- the child's welfare is paramount.

Reflective question

1. How have international perspectives influenced national child protection and safeguarding initiatives?

The United Nations General Assembly (UNGA) adopted the *Declaration of the Rights of the Child* in 1959, laying the foundation for the UNCRC, which was established in 1989. Today, the UNCRC is the most comprehensive and legally binding international agreement on children's rights. It has been ratified by 196 countries, including the United Kingdom, making it the most widely ratified human rights treaty in history. The only UN member state that has not ratified the convention is the US (UNICEF, 2024b).

United Nations Convention on the Rights of the Child (UNCRC)

Containing a total of 54 articles, the UNCRC includes 42 articles that specifically outline children's rights, with the remaining articles focused on implementation, monitoring and procedural mechanisms. The UNCRC provides a comprehensive framework addressing all aspects of children's lives, from health and education to protection and participation. The UN Committee on the Rights of the Child encourages governments at all levels to use the convention as a foundation for policy-making and implementation (UNICEF, 2024b).

The UNCRC has significantly shaped both global and national child protection policies. In the UK, its influence is evident in the establishment of the Office of the Children's Commissioner, created under the Children Act 2004 following the Victoria Climbié Inquiry (Laming, 2003), to represent the views and interests of children. In contrast to the UK, some countries have fully embedded the UNCRC into domestic law. For example, Norway incorporated the convention through its Human Rights Act 2003, granting it precedence over conflicting national legislation. This ensures that the UNCRC is directly applicable and enforceable in Norwegian courts. Also, in Sweden, the UNCRC was incorporated into national law in 2020 (Stern, 2021). Sweden's move towards direct incorporation of the convention was driven by the recognition that, despite strategic initiatives, the UNCRC had not sufficiently influenced the practices of central and local governments (UNICEF, n.d.a). These examples have set a precedent for other ratifying nations, including the UK, to consider how incorporating the UNCRC into domestic law could strengthen mechanisms to promote children's rights.

Activity 1.4: The global ratification of the UNCRC

Reflect on the widespread ratification of the UNCRC and consider the following questions.

1. What shared values do you believe have motivated so many countries around the world to ratify the UNCRC?
2. How might the UNCRC's comprehensive framework for children's rights have influenced nations to ratify the convention? Consider the holistic approach reflected in its articles, which address a breadth of children's rights.
3. In what ways do you think international pressure may have influenced countries to ratify the UNCRC? Reflect on the fact that the US remains the only UN member state that has not fully ratified the convention.

The UNCRC has therefore been instrumental in influencing international child protection policies, including those within the UK. However, while this international framework is beneficial for setting global standards and encouraging cross-national collaboration, it may lead to the neglect of nationally contextualised approaches to child protection and safeguarding. Each country has unique social, cultural and economic factors that influence the implementation and effectiveness of child protection measures. By focusing heavily on international standards, there is a risk of overlooking country-specific factors (such as those discussed earlier in the chapter), which are crucial for developing tailored strategies that address local needs and conditions. Therefore, while the international framework is important, it must be complemented by robust, context-specific national approaches to effectively address children's rights issues. This need for tailored strategies may go some way in helping to explain why the UK, along with many other countries worldwide, still has considerable progress to make in fulfilling its obligations as a signatory of the UNCRC (see United Nations, 2023).

Sustainable Development Goals (SDGs)

Building on the UNCRC, the global community has also integrated child protection into broader agendas, such as the SDGs. Adopted in 2015 by all UN member states, the 17 SDGs aim to address the economic, social and environmental dimensions of sustainable development by 2030. The UNCRC aligns closely with the SDGs, particularly in their shared commitment to ending violence against children. SDG Target 16.2, under Goal 16: Peace, Justice and Strong Institutions, explicitly calls for the end of abuse, exploitation, trafficking and all forms of violence and torture against children by 2030. Taken together, the UNCRC and SDGs form a powerful framework for advancing children's rights globally. Beyond Goal 16, the UNCRC and SDGs intersect in multiple areas, such as:

- SDG 1: No Poverty – *Article 27* of the UNCRC affirms every child's right to a standard of living adequate for their physical, mental, spiritual, moral and social development
- SDG 2: Zero Hunger – *Article 24* highlights children's right to nutritious food

- SDG 4: Quality Education – *Articles 28 and 29* emphasise the right to education and the development of a child's personality, talents and abilities to their fullest potential
- SDG 5: Gender Equality – *Article 2* of the UNCRC prohibits discrimination on any grounds, including gender.

To a certain degree, the UNCRC 's obligations therefore inform and support the broader objectives of the SDGs, highlighting how children's rights are central to global efforts to achieve a better and more sustainable future for all. However, it has been observed that the mechanisms designed to implement the SDGs often lack sensitivity to, or compliance with, child rights. These mechanisms may not adequately address or prioritise the specific needs and protections required for children, potentially undermining the effectiveness of the SDGs in safeguarding and advancing children's rights (Nolan, 2020). Despite UNICEF's efforts to align the SDGs with the UNCRC (UNICEF, 2020a), the SDGs themselves do not intuitively reflect the children's rights agenda. As a result, they are often perceived as political statements or charitable appeals rather than legal commitments (Kilkelly, 2020). It is hardly surprising, therefore, that the latest data on progress against the SDG indicators shows limited progress to date. For example, according to the 2023 progress report, none of the indicators for Goal 16 appear to be on track, nor has the desired target for this SDG been met (UNDP, 2023). However, by recognising child protection within the SDGs, we can, at the very least, envision a future where global efforts continue to strive towards eradicating child abuse worldwide.

Activity 1.5: SDGs

The goal to end all forms of child abuse by 2030, as outlined in SDG 16.2, clearly remains a work in progress. Given this context, answer the following questions.

1. How likely do you think it is that this vision will be achieved globally by 2030?
2. How far do you think the UK has progressed in working towards this goal?
3. In what ways do you think the UK can improve its efforts to contribute to the prevention of child abuse to help achieve this goal?

Summary

This chapter has considered child abuse on a global level and has highlighted how cultural and economic factors influence the prevalence and nature of abuse. Cultural practices can either offer protection to children or expose them to harm, while economic inequalities can lead to abusive situations. However, it is essential to note that poverty does not necessarily lead to abuse. Many families living in poverty do not abuse or neglect their children, and factors such as over-surveillance, systemic racism and parental mental health issues also contribute to the complexities surrounding child maltreatment. Addressing child abuse globally, therefore, requires a nuanced understanding of intersecting factors and social identities which affect children's experiences.

This chapter has also explored the UNCRC, which plays a substantial role in shaping international child protection policies, including those in the UK. While the UNCRC sets high standards for the global community and promotes international cooperation, it can overshadow the need for country-level, context-specific understandings related to child abuse and child protection. Each country must therefore adapt the international standards to align with its unique legal, cultural and social context, as the practical application of the UNCRC requires localised adaptation and implementation. The SDGs go hand in hand with the UNCRC and integrate child protection principles into the broader agenda of global development. Goal 16.2 within the SDGs directly calls for the end of all forms of abuse towards children by 2030. While this goal may seem idealistic in today's reality, it provides a clear statement about the unacceptability of child abuse, with the hope of eradicating child maltreatment on a global level in the future.

2

Child abuse and the UK policy context

Introduction

The legal and policy landscape surrounding child abuse in the UK has developed over more than a century, shaped by changing social attitudes and understandings of what constitutes harm towards children. Each stage of this development reflects the growing recognition of children's rights and the need for more effective safeguarding measures. This chapter traces the legislative journey of child protection, from early statutes through to contemporary frameworks, and outlines how definitions of child abuse have broadened from physical, sexual, emotional abuse and neglect to include witnessing domestic abuse, and abuse in online and extra-familial contexts.

Additionally, the chapter highlights the role of feminism, children's rights advocacy, the media and public inquiries in shifting public discourse on child abuse and examines how the concept of historic abuse has emerged more recently. By considering inquiries into child abuse, the chapter illustrates how past injustices are increasingly being recognised as concerns for the present day. Through a historical and conceptual lens, social workers are encouraged to reflect on the evolving meanings of child abuse and their ongoing responsibilities in addressing both contemporary and historic harms.

Child protection legislation in England: a chronology

Child protection legislation in England has evolved significantly over time, shaped by shifting social attitudes and a growing understanding of the complexities of maltreatment. The following chronology briefly outlines key legislative developments both before and after the devolution of powers in the UK from 1998.

Infant Life Protection Act 1872: The term 'baby farming' was used in the 1860s to describe situations where women were paid to care for children who were not their own (Arnot, 1994). The Infant Life Protection Act of 1872 focused on the protection of infants who were placed in the care of others, by introducing regulations for the licensing and inspection of baby farms and similar establishments.

Prevention of Cruelty to, and Protection of, Children Act 1889: The Act allowed the state to intervene in parent–child relationships for the first time. The police gained the authority to charge individuals who mistreated children and to enter homes if a child was believed to be in danger. The Act also established regulations for child labour and prohibited begging.

Children Act 1908: The 1908 Act consolidated and extended earlier child protection laws. It introduced juvenile courts to deal separately with children accused of crimes, and established borstals for young offenders to replace adult prisons. The Act also abolished the death penalty for children under 16, restricted harmful forms of child labour and increased the responsibilities of local authorities for child welfare and protection.

Children and Young Persons Act 1933: The 1933 Act aimed to consolidate existing child protection legislation into a single statute. It brought together earlier laws relating to child welfare, juvenile justice and employment, and set out clearer definitions of child cruelty and neglect. It also raised the minimum age of execution to 18 and increased the minimum age for criminal responsibility from seven to eight years.

Children Act 1948: The Children Act 1948 emphasised the duty of local authorities to support children who were without parental care or in need. It introduced provisions for the assumption of parental rights by local authorities, laying the foundations for the concept of corporate parenting. The Act was largely influenced by the findings of the Curtis Committee (Report of the Care of Children Committee, 1946), following public concern about the poor state of institutional care.

Children and Young Persons Act 1963: This Act extended the powers of local authorities to promote the welfare of children. It placed a duty on them to offer guidance, advice and assistance to young people, either directly or through voluntary organisations (Stone, 1964). It also made provisions around care proceedings and the removal of children from harmful situations.

Children Act 1989: A landmark piece of legislation, the Act introduced reforms to child welfare practices in the UK and emphasised the welfare of children being paramount. The legislation established the framework for modern day child protection services including measures to protect children from abuse and neglect. The Children Act 1989 introduced the concept of *significant harm* as the threshold justifying compulsory intervention in family life in the best interests of children.

The Protection of Children Act 1999: This Act required the creation of a list (commonly known as List 99) of individuals deemed unsuitable to work with children. It allowed employers in childcare organisations to check potential employees against this list, forming part of safer recruitment practices in child-focused organisations.

Adoption and Children Act 2002: This Act updated the Children Act 1989 to reflect modern understandings of adoption and child welfare. It recognised that children could suffer significant harm not only through direct abuse, but also by witnessing domestic violence. The Act aligned adoption law more closely with the welfare principles of the Children Act 1989 and placed the child's welfare at the centre of all adoption decisions.

Sexual Offences Act 2003: This Act introduced a range of offences related to child sexual exploitation (CSE), including causing or inciting a child to engage in sexual activity. The legislation recognised that any sexual activity involving children under 16 is unlawful, even if seemingly consensual. Although the term 'child sexual exploitation' was not yet widely used, the Act laid important groundwork for its later recognition in policy and practice.

Children Act 2004: The Children Act 2004 followed the *Every Child Matters* green paper (DfES, 2003) and was largely a response to the Victoria Climbié Inquiry. It aimed to improve the integration, accountability and coordination of children's services. The Act required local authorities to appoint a director of children's services, established the Children's Commissioner for England and replaced area child protection committees with statutory local safeguarding children boards (LSCBs). It also provided a legal basis for improved information sharing across agencies.

Safeguarding Vulnerable Groups Act 2006: This Act created a new framework for vetting individuals who worked with children and vulnerable adults. It established the Independent Safeguarding Authority (ISA), which was responsible for maintaining barred lists and overseeing decisions about individuals' suitability to work in regulated settings.

Protection of Freedoms Act 2012: This Act scaled back the vetting and barring scheme to focus on roles with direct and regular contact with children and vulnerable adults, creating the Disclosure and Barring Service (DBS) to merge the functions of the ISA and the Criminal Records Bureau (CRB).

Children and Families Act 2014: This legislation included reforms for the adoption process, special educational needs support and family justice. Aimed at improving the welfare and safeguarding of children, it emphasised the importance of early intervention support for families and promoted stability and permanence for children looked after by the local authority.

Serious Crime Act 2015: This Act included a key provision that made emotional abuse and the persistent neglect of a child a criminal offence. It updated the offence of child cruelty under the 1933 Act to reflect a broader understanding of harm, including psychological and emotional harm.

Children and Social Work Act 2017: This Act improved support for looked after and previously looked after children, including care leavers. It replaced LSCBs with new multiagency safeguarding arrangements and established Social Work England (SWE) as the new regulator for social workers. It also introduced a duty to make *relationships education* compulsory in primary schools and *relationships and sex education* (RSE) compulsory in secondary schools in England, which was implemented in 2020.

Domestic Abuse Act 2021: Building on the provisions within the Adoption and Children Act of 2002, the Domestic Abuse Act 2021 recognised children as victims of domestic abuse in their own right, if they witnessed abusive behaviour towards a parent or relative.

The evolution of child protection legislation in England reflects a growing recognition of the need to protect children from all forms of harm and to intervene when necessary. These legislative developments have been pivotal in establishing a framework for safeguarding children and responding to child abuse in the present day.

Activity 2.1: Child protection legislation

Select one piece of historical legislation from the chronology (e.g., Infant Life Protection Act 1872, Children Act 1908) and reflect on the following questions.

a. How might prevailing social attitudes towards children have influenced the development of this legislation at the time, and in what ways might the legislation have contributed to shifting public perceptions of child protection in that historical context?
b. What challenges would practitioners or authorities at the time have faced in implementing this legislation, particularly in light of the dominant social norms, values and institutional structures of the period?
c. In what ways does this legislation continue to shape or inform contemporary social work practice in the field of child protection?

Defining 'child abuse' within the UK

The concept of child abuse is recognised as subjective and relative (Stainton-Rogers, 2001) and its meaning is susceptible to change over time (Ferguson, 2007; Parton, 2006). This complexity is further compounded by growing awareness that understandings of 'abuse' are inextricably linked to the cultural context in which they occur (Corby et al., 2012; Fontes, 2005; Korbin, 2002). Additionally, technological advances have contributed to expanding definitions of abuse to include activities that take place online (Page et al., 2025). This raises important questions about how child abuse is defined within legal and policy frameworks.

The UK is governed by overarching legislation passed by the UK Parliament at Westminster that can apply across the four nations. However, the introduction of additional, localised legislation and policies are matters for devolved administrations.

Since the devolution settlements of the late 1990s, Northern Ireland, Scotland and Wales have had the authority to develop their own legal and policy frameworks in areas such as education, health and social care – which are key domains for child protection. In the UK, therefore, definitions of child abuse appear in policies specific to each nation.

The Cruelty to, and Protection of, Children Act 1889 was the first major UK legislation aimed at protecting children from abuse and neglect. Chapter 44 of the Act defined child cruelty as:

> *If any person who has attained the age of sixteen years and has responsibility for any child or young person under that age, wilfully assaults, ill-treats, neglects, abandons, or exposes him, or causes or procures him to be assaulted, ill-treated, neglected, abandoned, or exposed, in a manner likely to cause him unnecessary suffering or injury to health … that person shall be guilty of a misdemeanour, and shall be liable.*

After a series of legislative developments over the course of the century (see chronology), the Children Act 1989 built upon existing definitions and linked the notion of abuse to the concept of *harm*. Harm, under Section 31 (9) of the Children Act 1989 is defined as the 'ill-treatment or the impairment of health or development'. Subsequently, Section 120 of the Adoption and Children Act 2002, expanded this definition by explicitly including, 'impairment suffered from seeing or hearing the ill-treatment of another'.

In interpreting the legislative definition, current statutory guidance within England defines child abuse as:

> *A form of maltreatment of a child. Somebody may abuse or neglect a child by inflicting harm, or by failing to act to prevent harm. Harm can include ill treatment that is not physical as well as the impact of witnessing ill treatment of others. This can be particularly relevant, for example, in relation to the impact on children of all forms of domestic abuse, including where they see, hear, or experience its effects. Children may be abused in a family or in institutional or extra-familial contexts by those known to them or, more rarely, by others. Abuse can take place wholly online, or technology may be used to facilitate offline abuse. Children may be abused by an adult or adults, or another child or children.*
>
> (DfE, 2023, p. 154)

In Wales, the *All Wales Child Protection Procedures 2008* (Welsh Assembly Government, 2008, p. 31) define child abuse and neglect as:

> *A child is abused or neglected when somebody inflicts harm, or fails to act to prevent harm. Children may be abused in a family or in an institutional or community setting, by those known to them or, more rarely, by a stranger.*

Similarly, in Scotland, the *National Guidance for Child Protection in Scotland 2014* (Scottish Government, 2014, p. 11) states that:

> *Abuse and neglect are forms of maltreatment of a child. Somebody may abuse or neglect a child by inflicting, or by failing to act to prevent, significant harm to the child. Children may be abused in a family or in an institutional setting, by those known to them or, more rarely, by a stranger.*

In terms of Northern Ireland, Article 2(2) of the Children (Northern Ireland) Order 1995 uses the word 'harm', to refer to the 'ill-treatment or the impairment of health or development including, for example, impairment suffered from seeing or hearing the ill-treatment of another'.

Additionally, the Safeguarding Board for Northern Ireland (2012) states:

> *Child abuse occurs when a child is neglected, harmed or not provided with proper care. Children may be abused in many settings, for example, in a family, in an institutional or community setting, by those known to them, or more rarely, by a stranger. There are different types of abuse and a child may suffer more than one of them.*

While the core principle that harm to children constitutes abuse has remained constant, legal frameworks have progressively expanded to encompass both active and passive acts, alongside increasingly nuanced understandings of maltreatment. Accordingly, notions of what is or is not acceptable for children to be exposed to have been socially and legislatively constructed and reconstructed across the UK over the past century. Although the Cruelty to, and Protection of, Children Act 1889 first established legal prohibitions against child ill treatment, societal thresholds for acceptable childhood experiences have undergone significant change.

Activity 2.2: Evolving understandings of physical abuse

The physical abuse of children provides one example of how socio-legal debates about what constitutes abuse have evolved, particularly in relation to notions of corporal punishment and physical chastisement. In UK law, *physical chastisement* and *corporal punishment* are often used interchangeably, but they can carry slightly different connotations in legal and social contexts (Rowland et al., 2017). Questioning the acceptability of specific forms of abuse historically, Smith (2008) highlights how what was considered everyday practice in the past is now considered abusive, particularly in relation to what falls within present understandings of physical abuse. For such reasons, the matter of what was or was not acceptable practice and whether historic acts of abuse, as per modern day definitions, should be considered abuse at all remains a contested matter. This reflects the ongoing controversy surrounding corporal punishment/physical chastisement in the UK over the last century, as societal thresholds of acceptability for these practices have shifted significantly over time. In research from the 1970s, Gil (1975, p. 352) found that 'the use of force towards children is widespread in our society on the institutional and family levels', and this was of concern.

Yet despite this recognition of harm, some degree of physical chastisement remains legally acceptable in England today, although Section 58 of the Children Act 2004 restricted the reasonable chastisement defence, preventing its use when individuals face charges involving bodily harm or cruelty against children. The widespread use of corporal punishment/physical chastisement during the twentieth century has consequently diminished, with clearer legal parameters now established regarding its acceptable limits. The Cruelty to, and Protection of, Children Act 1889 Act explicitly prohibited the wilful assault of children, yet the social acceptability of corporal punishment and physical chastisement over the years has created significant ambiguity. Historically, the legislation appeared to focus on intent rather than impact, but this approach was later amended as the harm caused to children by such practices has been recognised. This has likely influenced how, in Scotland, the Children (Equal Protection from Assault) (Scotland) Act 2019 has changed the law and removed the reasonable chastisement defence since November 2020, whereby children now have the same legal protection from assault as adults do. This stands in stark contrast to England, where the continued legal tolerance of physical chastisement remains a significant barrier to achieving full parity in children's rights protections (Rowland et al., 2017).

Question

1. Based on this case example, can you think of how definitions of other forms of child abuse may have evolved?

Defining 'historic abuse' within the UK

Building on the understanding of how child abuse is defined in the UK, the following section extends this discussion to the concept of *historic* abuse. The evolution in defining recent abuse provides a foundation for understanding the additional challenges present in considering abuse which occurred in the past. 'Historic abuse' is a value laden term (Hawthorn, 2006) and is often used interchangeably with other terms such as 'historical abuse', 'non-recent abuse' or 'past abuse'; and includes actions that occurred in the past but continue to impact victims/survivors in the present. Conceptually, therefore, it presents a unique challenge, due to the passage of time, changes in social norms and the evolution of legal standards.

Background

Concerns regarding historic abuse have reached heightened prominence within the UK, illustrated by the national inquiries which have been undertaken in England and Wales, Northern Ireland and Scotland, with a view to investigating past abuses. The launch of such inquiries has neither been a coincidental nor impromptu phenomenon; in fact they have been preceded by a range of developments and initiatives which ensured that historic abuse remained on the political agenda, ultimately leading to the launch of national investigations (Karim, 2020).

Historically, child abuse was understood through a lens that set much higher thresholds for what was considered to be harmful behaviour towards children, as compared to today's standards (DoH, 1995; Jenks, 2005). Over time, however, this perspective has evolved, leading to a more nuanced and comprehensive understanding of what constitutes abusive behaviour. This evolution can be traced back to key developments during the 1960s, a period that marked a turning point in how child abuse was recognised and responded to (Powell and Scanlon, 2014). These historical shifts laid the foundation for the contemporary concept of historic abuse to emerge, whereby a broader range of harmful actions that were often overlooked or tolerated in the past would be addressed in the present day.

The reduced power held by children compared to adults was a significant factor throughout the twentieth century, with children often seen as dependent on adults in their lives (Stein, 2006). Initially, the focus was predominantly on abuse within the family context, but the latter half of the century brought about significant changes in how children were understood and treated within the UK (Elsley, 2017), gradually addressing some of these power imbalances. Key developments during this period, such as the feminist movement (Whittier, 2009), legislative reforms, a new understanding of children's rights as articulated in the UNCRC (1989) and the role of the media in bringing these issues to light (Powell and Scanlon, 2014) were pivotal in reshaping social attitudes towards child protection.

The feminist movement: The feminist movement within the 1970s and 1980s was instrumental in bringing the physical and sexual abuse of children to the forefront of public consciousness in an unprecedented way (Delap, 2015; Whittier, 2009). This movement not only highlighted the rights of women, but also advocated for the rights of other marginalised groups, including children, with its critique on child abuse, power and patriarchy evolving through the 1990s (Seymour, 1998).

Activity 2.3: Feminism and the evolution of child abuse discourse

Reflective questions

1. To what extent has the feminist movement shaped contemporary understandings of child abuse?
2. How do its historical contributions continue to inform current child protection frameworks?

Children's rights to protection: This period of activism coincided with significant legislative reforms, most notably the Children Act 1989 which introduced a comprehensive framework for the protection and care of children in the UK (Aldgate and Hill, 1995). The Act was a landmark in child welfare legislation, emphasising the importance of safeguarding children's rights and wellbeing. Additionally, the UNCRC, ratified by the UK in 1990, further articulated the rights of children, recognising their right to protection from all forms of abuse (UNCRC, 1989).

Activity 2.4: Children's rights

Reflective questions

1. How did the Children Act 1989 and the ratification of the UNCRC in 1990 reflect a shift in how children's rights and welfare were understood and prioritised in the UK?
2. In what ways do these initiatives continue to influence contemporary social work practice in terms of promoting and protecting children's rights?

The role of the media: It is recognised that up until the mid-1980s victims/survivors often encountered difficulties in talking about the abuse they had suffered, largely due to the culture of silence around child abuse, along with the absence of a framework for thinking through or speaking of such traumatic events. However, as the media began to expose child abuse as a significant social issue, a new space was created where victims/survivors could begin to voice their experiences (Kitzinger, 2004). As awareness of child abuse grew, attention shifted from focusing solely on familial abuse to include children under state care, in relation to which, the term 'historic abuse' first emerged.

Activity 2.5: Media representations and public perceptions of child abuse

Reflective questions

1. To what extent has media coverage amplified understandings of child abuse?
2. How does the media influence current discussions around child protection?

Definitions of historic abuse

Although it is difficult to pinpoint the exact first use of the term 'historic abuse' within the UK context, notions of historic abuse emerged as part of the Waterhouse Inquiry, which started in 1996 and investigated alleged abuse in children's care settings in North Wales. The inquiry report included recognition of child abuse that had occurred years earlier (from 1974 onwards) which was of concern in the present day as:

> *Widespread sexual abuse of boys occurred in children's residential establishments in Clwyd between 1974 and 1990. There were some incidents of sexual abuse of girl residents in these establishments, but they were comparatively rare.*
>
> (DoH, 2000, p. 788)

Over the years, and through the course of local and national child abuse inquiries in the UK, there has been a growing recognition that cases of child abuse from the past need to be addressed, as the impact of historic abuse is understood to impact throughout peoples' lives (Horwitz et al., 2001). The concept of historic abuse has consequently become both clearer and more widely understood. In the UK, the NSPCC (2024a), states that, 'Non-recent child abuse, sometimes called historical abuse, is when an adult was abused as a child or young person under the age of 18.' While the Criminal Injuries Compensation Authority UK (CICA) defines historical abuse as:

> *Sometimes called non-recent abuse, historical abuse is defined as when an adult has been abused in the past when they were a child or under the age of 18. Some adults may have always known about the abuse while for others, it could be a recent understanding of what they went through.*
>
> (CICA, n.d.)

In Scotland specifically, within the *National Guidance for Child Protection*, historic abuse is defined as:

> *allegations of neglect, emotional, physical and sexual abuse which took place before the victim was 16 (or 18, in particular circumstances) and which have been made after a significant time lapse. The complainant may be an adult but could be an older young person making allegations of abuse in early childhood. The allegations may relate to an individual's experience in the family home, community or while a looked-after and accommodated child in a residential, kinship or foster care setting.*
>
> (Scottish Government, 2014)

The above definition from the Scottish government expands on the multifaceted nature of historical abuse and acknowledges its occurrence across different settings and time periods. Academically, however, such definitions have been critiqued, as allegations of abuse have not necessarily been made after a significant time lapse. In fact, there is evidence to suggest that children did speak of their abuse at the time it occurred and attempted to report their experiences, but that these disclosures were not always responded to in the way in which they should have been (Karim, 2017). Therefore, it is suggested that a more fitting definition would include recognition of how often disclosures were made, but such disclosures have been brought to the fore, following a significant time lapse (Karim, 2020), on the basis of which the following definition is suggested:

> *Historical abuse is the physical, sexual, emotional/psychological abuse or neglect experienced by children in the non-recent past, whereby disclosures of the abuse surfaced after a significant time lapse.*

In conclusion, the meaning of historic abuse has developed over time through public inquiries, official definitions and academic debate. While some definitions are based on the delay between when the abuse occurred and when it is reported, research identifies that victims often tried to speak out at the time but were not listened to. Understandings of historic abuse should therefore include a recognition of both the time that has passed and the fact that many disclosures were ignored or not acted upon when they were first made.

Case study 2.1

Edith's experience of historic abuse

Background

Edith is a 54-year-old female who recently disclosed that she was sexually abused by a friend of the family named Marcus when she was between ten and eleven years of age. Marcus was a close friend of Edith's parents and therefore often visited the family home. Edith is able to remember the abuse clearly, despite the time which has passed and she recalls trying to speak to her mother about it when she was younger. Edith's mother had dismissed what Edith was saying at the time by telling her 'not to make up stories'.

Following this experience, Edith became silent and chose not to speak about it any further due to the fear of not being believed and the confusion that her mother's response had created for her, which led her to believe that she may have been responsible in some way for what had happened.

As Edith became an adult, she repressed the memories of the abuse for many years as she tried to live what she considered to be a 'normal life'. However, when Edith's husband passed away in his early 50s, Edith was left alone as the couple did not have any children. Following this loss, Edith started experiencing a series of panic attacks and struggled with anxiety and depression which impacted her severely. She was referred for counselling through her GP and subsequently started accessing therapeutic support, where memories of the abuse resurfaced. Feeling encouraged by her therapist, Edith decided to report the abuse to the police. However, her case was complicated by the fact that Marcus was now elderly and living in a care home, and there was no physical evidence available to substantiate the allegations.

The police took Edith's disclosure of abuse very seriously, but had to inform her that pursuing legal action through the courts would be challenging due to the lack of evidence and the time which had passed since the abuse occurred. As a result, Edith felt a deep sense of injustice and shame, believing that her experiences were not being validated and the abuse that occurred was being minimised because it happened in the past. Edith also experienced guilt and blamed herself for not going to the police sooner and felt inadequate for not having the courage to speak about this at the time it occurred, despite her mother's inappropriate response.

Reflective questions

1. How does Edith's case support or challenge definitions of historic abuse? Should definitions of historic abuse be broader? What should such definitions include?
2. How might social workers advocate for justice when legal action poses a challenge due to the passage of time for victims/survivors of historic abuse?
3. How can social workers help manage the tension between the victim's/survivor's need for validation and the legal system's need for evidence?
4. How can social work practice help victims/survivors of abuse reconcile with the fact that formal justice may not be possible?
5. What other forms of closure or healing can be facilitated through social work intervention?

Summary

This chapter has provided an overview of the development of child protection legislation in the UK and specifically in England following devolution. It outlines how definitions of child abuse have expanded over time, moving beyond physical, sexual abuse and neglect, to include emotional harm, witnessing domestic violence, and abuse in online or extra-familial contexts. The chapter has also highlighted key shifts in legal thinking, from focusing on deliberate acts of harm to recognising the impact of inaction and indirect forms of abuse. These changes reflect broader shifts in social attitudes towards children and evolving understandings of harm and protection.

(Continued)

The chapter has explored the concept of historic abuse, explaining its emergence through inquiries into past abuse in children's care institutions. It also briefly considered how feminism, children's rights advocacy and media attention helped bring past abuses into public view and challenged the culture of silence that had previously existed. Definitions of historic abuse across the UK are also compared, and the chapter argues for a broader understanding that acknowledges disclosures which were ignored or dismissed in the past. With the development of legislation, the evolving definitions of child abuse and the increasing acknowledgement of historic abuse, it remains critical for social workers to continually integrate new knowledge into their practice; as despite the advancements, many challenges remain.

3 Forms of child abuse

Introduction

At its core, child abuse represents an abuse of power, where children are subjected to harm by individuals who are able to exercise power over them. This power dynamic can be exploited across all settings, from households to institutions, where perpetrators leverage their power to abuse children. Understanding child abuse through the lens of power is therefore critical to understanding its complexities and addressing its root causes effectively.

> *Some argue that abuse of power is central to defining different physical, sexual and emotional acts as 'violence', and others may argue that inherent in each of these dyads are unequal power relationships which mean that a range of acts can be classified as 'violence'.*
>
> (Devries et al., 2018, p. 2)

With an acknowledgement of the role of power, therefore, this chapter examines the definitions and indicators of various forms of child abuse, including physical abuse, emotional/psychological abuse, sexual abuse, neglect and child sexual exploitation. It also explores broader concerns in the field of child protection, such as fabricated or induced illness (FII) and female genital mutilation (FGM). The chapter concludes by examining emerging understandings of online abuse within the UK context, focusing on categories of child abuse and exploitation which are known to occur through the use of technology, including the production and distribution of child sexual abuse materials (CSAM).

Abuse types, definitions and indicators

The previous chapter explored the concept of *child abuse* within the UK context, including its legal definitions, which describe it as a form of maltreatment, whereby somebody may abuse or neglect a child by inflicting harm, or by failing to act to prevent harm (DfE, 2023). To build on this foundational knowledge, understanding specific forms of child maltreatment and their potential indicators is also essential. However, the task is not as straightforward as it may seem, as forms of child abuse often overlap, making it crucial to consider a child's experiences holistically. For instance, a child subjected to physical abuse may also suffer emotional/psychological abuse, as the physical harm can lead to feelings of fear and humiliation. Similarly, sexual abuse can co-occur with physical abuse, as sexual abuse often involves physically abusive behaviours. Therefore, although the boundaries between types of abuse are often blurred, distinguishing between them provides a valuable foundation for understanding the different forms of harm children may experience.

Physical abuse

Physical abuse involves the intentional use of physical force against a child that results in, or has the potential to result in, physical injury (Norman et al., 2012). According to statutory guidance in the UK, physical abuse may involve, 'hitting, shaking, throwing, poisoning, burning, or scalding, drowning, suffocating, or otherwise causing physical harm to a child. Physical harm may also be caused when a parent or carer fabricates the symptoms of, or deliberately induces, illness in a child' (DfE, 2023, p. 160). Essentially, physical abuse is a way of exerting power over someone through the use of physical force; however, it can also appear in more subtle forms, as is the case with inducing or fabricating illness in a child. Other examples of physical abuse include:

- *using weapons*: inflicting harm with objects such as knives, guns, or other tools;
- *physical restraint*: holding or tying someone down to restrict their movement;
- *exposure to extreme temperatures*: subjecting someone to very hot or cold conditions;
- *sleep deprivation*: preventing someone from sleeping to cause harm.

According to the Crime Survey for England and Wales (CSEW), approximately 7.6 per cent of adults aged 18 to 74 reported experiencing physical abuse before the age of 16, equating to approximately 3.1 million individuals. This statistic refers to incidents where the perpetrators were aged 16 or over. In the year ending March 2019, police in England and Wales recorded 117,617 offences of child physical abuse. Additionally, as of

31 March 2019, there were 4,170 children in England on child protection plans (CPPs), specifically for experiencing or being at risk of physical abuse (ONS, 2019a), highlighting the prevalence of the issue.

Indicators of physical abuse

Signs of physical abuse are often visible on the child's body. These can include bruises, cuts, burns and broken bones. Physical abuse may present itself in patterns, often with the child displaying injuries in areas which are typically covered by clothing. As outlined by the NSPCC (2024b), common indicators of physical abuse include:

- frequent and unexplained injuries;
- injuries at different stages of healing;
- wearing inappropriate clothing, such as long sleeves in hot weather, to cover injuries;
- flinching from physical contact;
- exhibiting extreme behaviour (aggressive or overly passive).

Focus on power

Physical abuse typically involves the intentional use of physical force or power over another person. When adults physically abuse children the power imbalance present is particularly pronounced as children are physically smaller and less able to defend themselves. As a result, the exertion of power through physical abuse not only causes bodily harm, but also reinforces adult authority, leaving children both physically and psychologically disempowered.

Fabricated or induced illness

Often referred to as Munchausen syndrome by proxy, FII is recognised as a form of physical abuse and involves parents or carers deliberately causing, fabricating, or exaggerating symptoms of illness in a child. The motivations behind FII can vary and may include a desire for attention or sympathy, a need for support, or a distorted belief that the child is genuinely unwell (Jones, 2021; NHS, 2023). Research suggests that FII should be recognised as a serious form of child abuse, as it typically involves a sustained pattern of deceptive behaviour by caregivers (Nardello, 2017). However, the increasing numbers of FII allegations in the UK have raised concerns about power imbalances within the child protection system, where families often struggle to defend themselves against false accusations (Cerebra, 2023).

Female genital mutilation

Often abbreviated as FGM, female genital mutilation bridges between being a form of physical and sexual abuse. As necessary as it is, categorising different forms of child abuse presents challenges because the boundaries between various forms of maltreatment can often be blurred (Laajasalo et al., 2023), as illustrated by the practice of FGM.

According to the World Health Organization (2025), it is estimated that over 230 million girls and women worldwide have been subjected to FGM, primarily in countries across Africa, the Middle East, and Asia. In England and Wales, FGM is a criminal offence under the Female Genital Mutilation Act 2003. Yet, despite this legal protection, it is estimated that approximately 10,000 girls under the age of 15, 103,000 females aged 15–49 and 24,000 females aged 50 and over, who have migrated to England and Wales are living with the consequences of FGM (Home Office, 2020b). However, although FGM remains a critical safeguarding concern, recent research indicates that its prevalence in the UK may be significantly lower than what is reflected in official statistics. As a result, policies based on inflated estimates risk not only misrepresenting the scale of the issue, but also inadvertently stigmatising and harming girls and women from affected communities (Karlsen et al., 2023).

The World Health Organization (2025) classifies FGM into four main types.

- **Type 1. Clitoridectomy**: Partial or total removal of the clitoris and/or the prepuce (the fold of skin surrounding the clitoris).
- **Type 2. Excision**: Partial or total removal of the clitoris and the labia minora, with or without excision of the labia majora.
- **Type 3. Infibulation**: Narrowing of the vaginal opening by creating a covering seal. This is formed by cutting and repositioning the labia minora or labia majora, sometimes through stitching, with or without removal of the clitoris.
- **Type 4. Other harmful procedures**: Including all other harmful procedures to the genital area for non-medical reasons, such as piercing, scraping, or cauterising.

FGM is a multifaceted issue situated at the intersection of culture, gender inequality and public health (UNICEF and UNFPA, 2018). For social workers, therefore, it is crucial to understand the cultural context, gender dynamics and the health-related consequences of FGM, particularly when working with migrant communities who may have been affected by the practice prior to settlement in the UK.

Sexual abuse

According to the Crime Survey for England and Wales (CSEW) approximately 7.5 per cent of adults aged 18 to 74 (equivalent to around 3.1 million people) reported having experienced sexual abuse before the age of 16. Additionally, in the year ending March 2019, police recorded 73,260 sexual offences involving child victims. During the same period, 2,230 children in England and 120 in Wales were placed on Child Protection Plans (CPPs) or registers due to either having experienced sexual abuse or being identified as at risk of such harm (ONS, 2019c).

Child sexual abuse (CSA) can be defined in different ways in different contexts (Mathews and Collin-Vézina, 2019); however, within statutory guidance from the UK CSA is understood to:

> *Involve forcing or enticing a child or young person to take part in sexual activities, not necessarily involving a high level of violence, whether or not the child is aware of what is happening. The activities may involve physical contact, including assault by penetration (for example, rape or oral sex) or non-penetrative acts, such as masturbation, kissing, rubbing,*

> *and touching outside of clothing. They may also include non-contact activities, such as involving children in looking at, or in the production of, sexual images, watching sexual activities, encouraging children to behave in sexually inappropriate ways, or grooming a child in preparation for abuse. Sexual abuse can take place online, and technology can be used to facilitate offline abuse. Sexual abuse is not solely perpetrated by adult males. Women can also commit acts of sexual abuse, as can other children.*
>
> (DfE, 2023, p. 162)

Based on the interpretation of the statutory definition, CSA may be classified into three distinct categories: physical, non-physical and exposure-related forms of sexual abuse.

Physical

- *Sexual assault*: this includes sexual acts such as penetration (rape, oral sex) or more severe non-penetrative acts.
- *Inappropriate touch*: any inappropriate touching, fondling, or groping of a child's intimate/private areas.

Non-physical

- *Grooming*: the process by which an adult builds a relationship with the child to lower their inhibitions and make them more vulnerable to sexual abuse.
- *Encouraging sexual behaviour*: encouraging or pressurising a child to behave in sexually inappropriate ways.
- *Online sexual abuse*: online sexual abuse involves the use of digital technologies or internet-enabled platforms to sexually exploit, groom, or abuse children.

Exposure

- *Exposure to sexual acts*: forcing or coercing a child to watch sexual acts or pornography.
- *Exposure to explicit content*: intentionally showing a child sexually explicit material (e.g., videos or pictures).

Understanding the full spectrum of child sexual abuse is essential for social workers tasked with safeguarding children. Recognising its varied forms enables more effective identification, intervention and support for those at risk or those who have already been affected.

Focus on power

Child sexual abuse frequently involves manipulation, threats and coercion as a means of exerting power and control over victims. Perpetrators often use intimidation to enforce silence, while instilling shame and guilt that further isolate the child. As a result, children may not disclose the abuse due to fear or embarrassment. This abuse of power not only silences victims, but also reinforces the perpetrator's control, often enabling the abuse to continue for prolonged periods of time.

Indicators of sexual abuse

CSA may be identified through a range of indicators; detailed guidance is available for professionals on recognising what these are (see CSA Centre, 2023). Some of the key indicators of sexual abuse are noted to be:

- genital or anal pain, bleeding or discharge;
- sexually transmitted infections;
- pregnancy;
- sexualised behaviour;
- premature sexual knowledge inconsistent with the child's developmental stage;
- creating sexually explicit drawings or written content;
- demonstrating a marked avoidance of physical contact or engaging in inappropriate forms of touch.

Case study 3.1

Peer sexual abuse

Liam (12) and Jake (16) attended the same all-boys secondary school and became acquainted through the school football team, where Jake, an older and more confident student, served as team captain. Liam, who was quieter and more reserved, looked up to Jake and was eager to earn his approval. Jake started paying considerable attention to Liam at school, which Liam thought was a sign of acceptance, making him increasingly vulnerable to Jake's influence. Over time, however, Jake began to isolate Liam from his friends and initiated sexual contact that Liam did not consent to. He used manipulation and subtle threats, such as warning Liam he would tell other students about what had happened to maintain control and ensure Liam's compliance.

As the sexual abuse escalated, Jake instilled feelings of shame and guilt in Liam, telling Liam that no one would believe him if he spoke out and that he would face embarrassment if he ever mentioned what was happening between them. As a result, Liam felt unable to tell anyone about the abuse, and remained silent about what he was being subjected to. The power imbalance, rooted in age, social status and coercion, therefore, allowed the sexual abuse to continue for months until Jake left the school to start college.

Reflective questions

1. How might power imbalances in peer relationships affect the likelihood of disclosure and the ability of professionals to intervene effectively?
2. What strategies can social workers use to build trust and create safe spaces for children to disclose abuse, particularly when the perpetrator is another young person?

Child sexual exploitation

The UK formally recognised *child sexual exploitation* (CSE) as a distinct category of abuse through the publication of statutory guidance on *Safeguarding Children and Young People from Sexual Exploitation* (DCSF, 2009) and, by 2017, CSE had been clearly established within safeguarding frameworks as a specific form of child sexual abuse.

> *Child sexual exploitation is a form of child sexual abuse. It occurs where an individual or group takes advantage of an imbalance of power to coerce, manipulate or deceive a child or young person under the age of 18 into sexual activity (a) in exchange for something the victim needs or wants, and/or (b) for the financial advantage or increased status of the perpetrator or facilitator. The victim may have been sexually exploited even if the sexual activity appears consensual. Child sexual exploitation does not always involve physical contact; it can also occur through the use of technology.*
>
> (DfE, 2017, p. 5)

The definition identifies the power imbalances present by highlighting how perpetrators can take advantage of their power position to exploit children who are inherently vulnerable. The definition also recognises how individuals or organised groups can perpetrate abuse, even where there may be perceived consent; as there is a level of coercion, manipulation or deceit involved in sexual exploitation which negates consent. By specifying that exploitation can occur in exchange for something, including money or status, the definition of CSE acknowledges the complexity of the victim's circumstances and how their needs can be manipulated by perpetrators. The risk of online CSE is also mentioned within the definition, aligning with findings that technological advancements have increased children's susceptibility to sexual exploitation in both offline and online environments (Livingstone et al., 2017).

Indicators of CSE

There are a range of indicators that may signal a child or young person is being sexually exploited, which include:

- acquiring money, clothing, mobile phones, etc., without a reasonable explanation;
- associating with gangs and/or being isolated from peers or social networks;
- having relationships with controlling or significantly older individuals;
- leaving home or care settings without explanation and/or consistently going missing or returning late;
- receiving an excessive number of texts or calls from unknown adults or peers;
- returning home under the influence of drugs or alcohol;
- engaging in age-inappropriate sexual behaviour or contracting sexually transmitted infections.

(DfE, 2017, p. 9)

Case study 3.2

Child sexual exploitation

Zuri, aged 15, was previously a happy and socially engaged teenager. However, recent changes in her behaviour raised significant concerns. She began staying out late, often not returning home until after midnight; when she did, she appeared distressed and under the influence of alcohol. Her mother also noticed that Zuri had acquired expensive

(Continued)

items, including a designer jacket and a high-end smartphone. When questioned, Zuri dismissed her mother's concerns, claiming the items were gifts from friends.

At school, Zuri's academic performance declined sharply. Once attentive and engaged, she became withdrawn and distracted, prompting concern from her teacher, Ms Nielson. During a one-to-one meeting with Ms Nielson, Zuri disclosed that she had recently been befriended by Shauna, an 18-year-old girl who introduced her to a group of older men. Initially, the men showered Zuri with gifts, money and attention, which made her feel special. However, after some weeks, the men began demanding sexual favours in exchange for the gifts they had given to her. They also introduced her to drugs and alcohol, which Zuri said she had become addicted to, further deepening her dependence and weakening her ability to say no to them. Zuri was extremely upset and shared that she felt trapped, ashamed and powerless, unable to see a way out of the situation.

Reflective questions

1. How did the adults involved take advantage of the power imbalance present to sexually exploit Zuri?
2. What safeguarding actions should follow a disclosure like Zuri's?

Emotional/psychological abuse

According to the CSEW, approximately one in 11 adults aged 18 to 74 years (around 3.8 million people) reported experiencing emotional abuse before the age of 16. Emotional abuse was the most common category of abuse on the Child Protection Register (CPR) in Wales, involving 1,295 children as of March 2019, and the second most common for CPPs in England, with 18,460 children affected. This marked an increase in cases of emotional abuse compared to previous years, in contrast to a decline in other forms of abuse (ONS, 2019b).

Emotional/psychological abuse refers to a broad spectrum of behaviours which impact on children's mental and emotional wellbeing. The statutory definition states how this form of abuse involves:

> *The persistent emotional maltreatment of a child so as to cause severe and persistent adverse effects on the child's emotional development. It may involve conveying to a child that they are worthless or unloved, inadequate, or valued only insofar as they meet the needs of another person. It may include not giving the child opportunities to express their views, deliberately silencing them, or making fun of what they say or how they communicate. It may feature age or developmentally inappropriate expectations being imposed on children. These may include interactions that are beyond a child's developmental capability, as well as overprotection and limitation of exploration and learning, or preventing the child participating in normal social interaction. It may involve seeing or hearing the ill-treatment of another. It may involve serious bullying (including cyber bullying), causing children frequently to feel frightened or in danger, or the exploitation or corruption of children. Some level of emotional abuse is involved in all types of maltreatment of a child, though it may occur alone.*
>
> (DfE, 2023, p. 157)

The definition of emotional abuse includes various harmful actions, such as making a child feel worthless, unloved, or inadequate. The broad scope of the definition highlights the multifaceted nature of emotional abuse and its presence across different forms of child maltreatment.

Activity 3.1

Emotional or psychological abuse?

The terms 'emotional abuse' and 'psychological abuse' are frequently used interchangeably because they both refer to the invisible harm caused to an individual's mental and emotional wellbeing. On the one hand, it is argued that distinguishing between psychological and emotional abuse is unhelpful, as cognition and emotion are closely intertwined (Glaser, 2002). On the other hand, it is suggested that differences exist between the two, with each term carrying slightly different connotations depending on the characteristics of the abuse (O'Hagan, 1995).

Consider the distinctions between emotional and physical abuse outlined below and answer the questions which follow.

Emotional abuse

- *Focus*: emotional abuse usually refers to actions that affect an individual's emotional state or wellbeing.
- *Characteristics*: it can include verbal attacks, humiliation, threats, rejection and excessive criticism which can lead to feelings of worthlessness, fear, or anxiety. Emotional abuse can also include isolating the victim from others or undermining their self-esteem.
- *Examples*: calling someone names, belittling them, making them feel worthless, ignoring or dismissing their feelings, or giving them the silent treatment.

Psychological abuse

- *Focus*: psychological abuse often involves behaviours that affect an individual's mind or cognitive processes, often aiming to destabilise or control their perception of reality.
- *Characteristics*: this type of abuse may involve gaslighting (manipulating someone into questioning their own reality), threats of harm, constant surveillance, or other behaviours that distort the victim's sense of self and/or perception.
- *Examples*: constantly making someone question their memory or sanity, threatening them or their loved ones with harm, or manipulating them into doubting their own judgement or experiences.

Reflective questions

1. What implications might the distinction between emotional and psychological abuse have for recognising and responding to different forms of harm?
2. How might the overlapping characteristics of emotional and psychological abuse affect the way such experiences are identified and understood in practice?
3. In what ways could a focus on either emotional or psychological aspects of abuse influence the types of support or interventions considered appropriate?

Indicators of emotional/psychological abuse

Emotional or psychological abuse can be more difficult to detect than physical forms of child maltreatment as it often requires careful observation of a child's emotional and psychological state. Children who are experiencing emotional abuse may present with the following signs:

- low self-confidence or a lack of self-assurance;
- difficulty regulating their emotions;
- challenges in forming or maintaining relationships;
- self-harming behaviours;
- persistent self-criticism or negative self-talk;
- the sudden onset of speech difficulties;
- repeated episodes of bedwetting or soiling;
- heightened sensitivity or disproportionate reactions to mistakes.

(Safeguarding Network, 2024)

Children's emotional/psychological development evolves with age, and signs of emotional/psychological abuse can vary depending on the child's developmental stage. Young children who are abused may exhibit behaviours such as excessive affection towards strangers or unfamiliar individuals. They may also appear insecure, nervous, or anxious in social settings and struggle to form close, trusting relationships with parents or caregivers. In some cases, they may express emotional distress through aggression or cruelty towards other children or animals. Older children may have difficulty managing their emotions, leading to outbursts or emotional volatility. They may also appear socially withdrawn and lack the interpersonal skills typically expected for their age (NSPCC, 2024b).

Case study 3.3

Emotional/psychological abuse

Lucia is a 14-year-old girl who attends secondary school and often appears isolated, with very few friends and limited social interactions. Lucia struggles to manage her emotions, frequently having outbursts at school ranging from tearfulness to anger. Her teachers have also observed that Lucia is reluctant to engage in group activities and has trouble connecting with her peers. She often appears withdrawn and anxious, and her responses to feedback can be overly defensive or emotional. Lucia rarely contributes to class discussions and tends to avoid eye contact, showing signs of low self-esteem and a lack of confidence in her abilities.

At home, Lucia's relationship with her mother is difficult. Her mother became a widow when Lucia was three and has suffered from depression ever since, while working long hours to make ends meet. For as long as she can remember, Lucia has found her mother to be emotionally unavailable, leaving Lucia to manage her own emotions. When Lucia tries to express herself or ask for support, her mother always dismisses her, criticising her for not being 'better behaved' or 'mature enough'. When frustrated, Lucia's mother tells her that she wishes Lucia had died instead of her father, so that she would have had support rather than the burden of raising an 'ungrateful child'. In addition to these hurtful remarks, Lucia is frequently blamed for things that go wrong at home, regardless of whether she is involved. Her mother often tells her that she is the reason for her unhappiness and failure in life. The constant criticisms and hurtful words from her mother have left Lucia feeling unworthy and unloved.

Reflective questions

1. What aspects of Lucia's mother's behaviour are emotionally/psychologically abusive?
2. How has Lucia's mother's behaviour potentially impacted on Lucia's emotional development?
3. How might Lucia's relationship with her mother have affected her ability to form relationships with other children at school?

Neglect

The term 'child abuse and neglect' (commonly abbreviated as CAN) is often used to describe child maltreatment, with neglect typically regarded as related to, but distinct from, other forms of abuse. This distinction is important as most forms of abuse involve harmful actions, whereas neglect is characterised by a failure to act. Specifically, neglect involves the omission of necessary care, protection, or attention that a child requires. In this sense, it reflects an absence of appropriate adult behaviour, rather than the presence of overtly abusive acts.

It is estimated that one in 100 adults aged 18 to 74 years experienced physical neglect before the age of 16, affecting approximately 481,000 individuals. This includes not being properly cared for or lacking sufficient food, shelter or clothing, but does not encompass all types of neglect. Neglect was also the most common reason for child protection plans in England, with 25,330 children under such plans as of 31 March 2019, and the second most common reason for children being placed on the CPR in Wales (ONS, 2021).

Within the UK, neglect has been defined as:

> *The persistent failure to meet a child's basic physical and/or psychological needs. Neglect may occur during pregnancy as a result of maternal substance abuse. Once a child is born, neglect may involve a parent or carer failing to provide adequate food, clothing, and shelter (including exclusion from home or abandonment), protect a child from physical and emotional harm or danger, ensure adequate supervision (including the use of inadequate caregivers), ensure access to appropriate medical care or treatment, provide suitable education. It may also include neglect of, or unresponsiveness to, a child's basic emotional needs.*
>
> (DfE, 2023, p. 160)

Indicators of neglect

In similar ways to emotional abuse, neglect may not have any obvious physical signs in some cases, especially when the neglect is connected to the emotional and psychological needs of children. However, the following indicators may suggest that a child is being physically neglected:

- inappropriate clothing or footwear;
- poor hygiene (e.g., the child is persistently smelly and/or dirty);
- untreated medical conditions (e.g., scabies or headlice);
- inadequate food provision (where the child is frequently hungry) leading to malnutrition;
- living in an unsafe or unclean environment;
- being abandoned.

(NICE, 2017)

Focus on power

Whereas child abuse manifests through the misuse of power via harmful actions (doing), neglect is characterised by the misuse of power through inaction (not doing) – that is, failing to provide children with essential care and support. Neglect is therefore not merely absence; it can be a choice to withhold necessities (whatever the reason may be), leaving the child powerless to meet their own needs.

Research indicates that, despite clear evidence linking neglect to a range of negative outcomes for children, it continues to be a lower priority for social work interventions compared to other forms of maltreatment (Gibbs et al., 2024). In part, this can be attributed to the difficulties present in determining the appropriate threshold for intervention, particularly in cases where neglect is cumulative. The inadequacy of current assessment tools to measure neglect contributes to the limited understanding of the issue as existing measures fail to capture its full complexity, leaving the evidence base too weak to effectively guide policy or practice (Haworth et al., 2024).

Case study 3.4

Neglect

Twelve-year-old Emily lives with both of her parents and two younger siblings. Although she attends school regularly, staff have become increasingly concerned about her wellbeing. Over the past year, signs of neglect have gradually emerged: Emily has been arriving late for school, appearing tired and showing signs of poor personal hygiene. Her clothes are frequently unwashed, her hair is unkempt and she often lacks appropriate clothing for the weather.

At home, both parents work long hours due to financial pressures. Emily's mother works full-time during the day while the children are at school, and her father works irregular shifts, often overnight or on weekends, and is frequently away from home. Although the children are technically supervised, Emily has taken on increasing responsibility for her younger siblings outside school hours, preparing meals, helping with homework and putting them to bed.

It is evident that Emily experiences a lack of consistent adult presence and support, as routines such as regular meals, clean clothing and help with schoolwork are often overlooked or left for her to manage. Staff at the school have noted that while the family appears to be doing their best under challenging circumstances Emily's wellbeing is increasingly compromised.

Reflective questions

1. What challenges arise in identifying and responding to neglect that develops gradually over time, and how can practitioners ensure that early indicators are not overlooked?
2. In cases where neglect is linked to underlying factors such as the need for parents to work, how can practitioners balance empathy for the family with the need to prioritise the child's wellbeing?

Online and technology-facilitated abuse

A growing body of literature recognises that various forms of harm perpetrated against children are increasingly facilitated through digital technologies. These harms encompass a wide range of abusive behaviours (sexual, emotional, psychological and economic) that often exploit the unique dynamics of the online environment. Due to the ongoing challenges in detecting and responding to emerging forms of harm which children may be exposed to through the use of technology, the UK's recent Online Safety Act 2023 includes numerous provisions specifically aimed at safeguarding children online. Protections contained within the Act require platforms to prevent access to harmful and/or age-inappropriate content. Additionally, it ensures that parents and children have accessible methods to report online issues as they arise (Online Safety Act, 2023). The Act specifies the categories of harmful content that platforms must protect children from. It mandates that children should be blocked from accessing *primary priority content* and allows for age-appropriate access to *priority content*. The types of content that fall into these categories are:

Primary priority content

- pornography;
- content that encourages, promotes, or provides instructions for either: self-harm, eating disorders or suicide.

Priority content

- abusive or hateful content;
- bullying;
- content which depicts or encourages serious violence or injury;
- content which encourages dangerous stunts and challenges;
- content which encourages the ingestion, inhalation or exposure to harmful substances.

(DSIT, 2023)

Forms of online harm

The following offers a brief overview of some of the categories of child abuse and exploitation which are known to occur through the use of technology.

- **Child sexual abuse materials (CSAM)**: Explicit content involving a child, which can include photographs, videos, or AI-generated images of children (IWF, 2025).
- **Cyberbullying**: The use of digital platforms to harass, threaten, or humiliate children. This includes sending harmful messages or sharing embarrassing images or videos (Vismara et al., 2022).
- **Exploitation via gaming**: Online gaming has introduced new avenues for child exploitation, including sexual exploitation, trafficking and financial abuse through in-game purchases or interactions with adult predators (Kavenagh, 2022).
- **Exposure to inappropriate content**: Children being exposed to age-inappropriate or harmful content, such as pornography, violence, or other disturbing material, through digital platforms (Wold et al., 2009).
- **Online grooming**: The process by which predators use digital platforms to build relationships with children to exploit or abuse them (NSPCC, 2025).
- **Online sexual exploitation**: The use of digital means to exploit children sexually, including sextortion, where victims are coerced into providing sexual images, videos, or money under the threat of exposing compromising material (NSPCC, 2025).
- **Radicalisation**: The process of using digital platforms to indoctrinate children with extremist ideologies or recruit them to participate in harmful activities (DfE, 2021a).
- **Virtual reality (VR) abuse**: Abuse which takes place within virtual reality environments, including verbal harassment, inappropriate physical interactions (such as inappropriate touching) and other actions intended to cause distress or discomfort to the child (Porta et al., 2023).

Ofcom's *Risk Assessment Guidance* (2024), developed under the Online Safety Act 2023, provides a structured framework for online services to identify, assess and mitigate risks of harm. Several of the priority areas listed, such as child sexual exploitation and abuse, grooming, child sexual abuse material (CSAM), harassment and threats, encouragement of suicide or self-harm, and exposure to hate offences can be understood as particularly relevant to the protection of children online.

Activity 3.2: AI-generated CSAM

The creation of AI-generated child abuse imagery is an emerging and increasingly serious concern in the UK. In 2024, for example, Hugh Nelson used artificial intelligence to manipulate innocent photographs of children, transforming them into explicit images which he then distributed for profit online (Gawne, 2024). In this case, the perpetrator used their technical knowledge to bypass protective measures and perpetrate harm remotely. This highlights the power disparity between the perpetrator and child victims, who may never be aware that their images have been used inappropriately; while the abuse can persist indefinitely online, beyond their knowledge or control. Nelson was subsequently sentenced to 18 years in prison for the production and distribution of these AI-generated indecent images. This case marked one of the first major prosecutions involving AI-generated abuse material and established a significant legal precedent: that such imagery would be treated with the same seriousness under the law as indecent photographs of real children (CPS, 2024).

Reflective questions

1. How can social workers contribute to preventing AI-facilitated child abuse before harm occurs?
2. How might child protection systems adapt to address the unique challenges of AI-generated CSAM?
3. How can social workers educate families about the risks of sharing children's images online while respecting parental autonomy?

Summary

Building on the previous chapter's exploration of child abuse as an evolving concept within the UK context, this chapter offered an overview of the key forms of abuse currently recognised in UK policy and practice. It began by outlining the definitions and indicators of physical, sexual, emotional/psychological abuse and neglect, as well as CSE, emphasising the often-overlapping nature of these harms and the power imbalances that underpin them. The chapter also discussed fabricated or induced illness (FII) and female genital mutilation (FGM).

Following this, the chapter highlighted the growing role of technology in enabling harm towards children, introducing online abuse as an area of increasing concern. It outlined key risks including online grooming, cyberbullying, exploitation through gaming platforms and the production of AI-generated CSAMs. Legal responses such as the Online Safety Act 2023 were also noted, emphasising the need for safeguarding approaches that remain alert to the evolving nature of abuse facilitated through digital technologies. By expanding awareness of both well-recognised and emerging forms of abuse, the chapter encourages practitioners to remain critically reflective, informed and adaptive in their efforts to protect children in an increasingly complex social and digital landscape.

4 The impact of child abuse

Introduction

Within the previous chapter, it was recognised that all forms of child abuse are expressions of power. It is therefore essential to consider how such exercises of power impact individuals in the long and short term, and society more broadly – after all, using power can have far-reaching consequences. Building on the discussion of abuse typologies from the preceding chapter, this chapter explores the potential impact of child abuse at multiple levels, both in the immediate aftermath and over time. While these effects manifest in diverse ways at the individual level, they also produce broader social and economic repercussions that extend beyond the person who was abused. Understanding these impacts is vital for social workers who support child or adult victims/survivors of abuse (see Chapters 8 and 9) as it equips practitioners with the insight needed to tailor interventions, advocate effectively and respond with sensitivity to the needs of those affected.

For this purpose, the chapter is divided into three parts. The first part examines the immediate impacts of child abuse on children's physical, emotional, cognitive and social development. The second part considers the long-term consequences in adulthood, including mental and physical health challenges, relationship difficulties and economic outcomes. The final part explores the wider societal impacts, such as intergenerational harm, economic costs and strain on public services. By acknowledging the impact of abusive behaviours at both the individual and societal levels, we are better able to understand why protecting children from harm is a collective responsibility.

The immediate impact of child abuse on children

The immediate effects of child abuse typically emerge while the abuse is ongoing or shortly thereafter and can vary depending on factors such as the type and severity of maltreatment, the child's age, resilience and personal circumstances. It is therefore crucial to recognise that the impact on each child may differ, but may include physical, psychological, relational and educational consequences.

Immediate physical impact on children

Physical abuse often results in the most visible impacts on children, including injuries such as bruises, fractures and burns. In severe cases, physical abuse can also lead to permanent disabilities or even death. Sara Sharif, a ten-year-old girl from the UK, was found dead in her home in Surrey in 2023. A postmortem examination showed how she had suffered extensive injuries, including bruising, bite marks, burns and fractures from being physically abused by her father and stepmother. In his call to the authorities when fleeing the UK, Sara's father said, 'It wasn't my intention to kill her, but I beat her up too much.' The news story highlighted how, during a search of the home, authorities discovered disturbing items, including a cricket bat stained with Sara's blood (Sandford, 2024). Such tragic incidents clearly highlight the need for earlier detection and efforts to prevent the physical abuse of children.

Alongside physical injuries, the immediate physical impact of abuse can also include the following:

- **pain and discomfort**: children who experience physical or sexual abuse often suffer from acute pain in specific areas of their body (depending on where an injury occurred), which can affect their ability to move, eat or sleep;
- **medical concerns**: injuries caused by physical or sexual abuse can lead to infections, internal bleeding or other medical complications. Children who have been sexually abused specifically may contract sexually transmitted infections (STIs) and experience reproductive health concerns (Bechtel, 2010);
- **developmental delays**: all forms of child abuse can interfere with a child's growth, which can include delays with the development of motor skills and speech. Research indicates that maltreated children often exhibit impaired motor development, with those exposed to sexual or physical abuse showing the highest rates of motor coordination deficits (Wade et al., 2017). Research has also shown that the development of language skills in children who have experienced abuse and/or neglect can be delayed in comparison to children who have not experienced maltreatment (Sylvestre et al., 2016).

Immediate emotional and psychological impact on children

Abuse can have immediate and profound psychological and emotional effects on children. The immediate psychological (thinking) and emotional (feeling) impact may manifest in different ways. Finkelhor et al. (2007) identified *poly-victimisation* as a critical aspect of child abuse. Their study found that many children experience multiple forms of abuse rather than isolated incidents, which in turn increases the risk of trauma – as a result of which, poly-victims are more likely to suffer from severe mental health issues.

Depression and anxiety related impacts are recognised to be common among children who have experienced abuse (Infurna et al., 2016), as abuse can lead to feelings of sadness, hopelessness and low self-esteem. Research shows that children who are abused or neglected have heightened anxiety and emotional reactivity (NRC, 2014), which may in turn lead to anxiety disorders, panic attacks and difficulty sleeping (Fucà et al., 2024). In severe cases, children who have been abused may exhibit signs of clinical depression, self-harming behaviours and suicidal attempts and ideation (Angelakis et al., 2020). Additionally, children who experience abuse may exhibit changes in mood, may show irritability, or may present with concentration difficulties. These psychological shifts can affect the way in which the child experiences themselves and/or others, while also impacting on their behaviour (Manly et al., 1994).

Immediate impact on children's relationships

Child abuse can impact significantly on a child's ability to form and maintain healthy relationships. Children who are abused may struggle with trusting others, which makes it difficult for them to form close relationships. Within social work, this is often described as children experiencing *attachment difficulties*. Children who are abused by parents or caregivers may develop *insecure* attachment styles, which can be insecure-avoidant (dismissive) or insecure-ambivalent (anxious/preoccupied). Children who demonstrate insecure-avoidant attachment styles are likely to avoid or ignore caregivers and appear overly independent for their age, while children who present as insecure-ambivalent are likely to show excessive dependency on caregivers while alternating between seeking closeness and resisting comfort (Bowlby, 1988). The impact of abuse on children's relationships may also lead to social isolation, whereby children spend more time alone which can exacerbate feelings of loneliness and depression (Elliot et al., 2005).

Immediate impact on children's education

Research consistently shows a clear connection between child abuse and academic outcomes, indicating that any form of maltreatment heightens the likelihood of experiencing educational challenges (Crozier and Barth, 2005). Such experiences can undermine cognitive development, resulting in difficulties with reading, comprehension and overall academic performance (Petersen et al., 2014). However, while abuse may hinder educational progress for some children, school attendance can also serve as a protective factor, helping to mitigate some of its adverse effects (Wilkinson and Bowyer, 2017).

In the UK, it is recognised that primary schools typically adopt one of two approaches: the child and family welfare approach, which emphasises the role of schools in safeguarding children both at home and within the school environment; or the educational attainment approach, which prioritises high academic achievement. This creates a challenge in balancing the drive for academic success with the need to support children who have experienced abuse. Instead of viewing child welfare and educational attainment as competing priorities, integrating both approaches could provide more holistic support and lead to better outcomes for vulnerable students (Ward et al., 2012).

The long-term impact of child abuse on adults

The impact of child abuse is rarely confined to the immediate aftermath of the experience; instead, its effects can evolve and develop over time. Early signs of impact may be visible soon after the abuse, but these initial effects can deepen and evolve into more complex challenges as individuals grow older. In some cases, the harm caused can result in life-long repercussions, including chronic physical health conditions, enduring mental health difficulties and broader social and economic disadvantages.

Here, we consider some of the ways in which childhood abuse may continue to affect individuals into adulthood. As we do so, it is essential to acknowledge that experiences of abuse and its impacts differ significantly from person to person. These impacts should therefore not be seen as inevitable outcomes, nor should they be used to pathologise victims/survivors. Instead, the following outline reflects the diverse ways in which individuals *may* be affected by the childhood trauma they experienced.

Long-term impact on adult mental health

One of the most commonly understood long-term effects of abuse is its impact on adult mental health and psychological wellbeing. Research has repeatedly shown that individuals who experience abuse during their childhood are at significantly higher risk of developing chronic mental health issues during adulthood (Macpherson et al., 2021). Some of the mental health concerns which may arise in the longer term include:

- **depression and anxiety**: childhood maltreatment significantly raises the likelihood of developing depression and anxiety in adulthood, with research clearly showing that a substantial proportion of adult depression and anxiety is attributable to such early life experiences (Li et al., 2016);
- **post-traumatic stress disorder (PTSD)**: some victims/survivors of child abuse may experience PTSD, a condition that can significantly disrupt everyday life. While symptoms often emerge within the first month of the traumatic event, they can also be delayed by months or even years. The severity and frequency of symptoms can vary, whereby some individuals may experience persistent distress, while others may go through alternating periods of stability and heightened distress.

  PTSD symptoms generally fall into three broad categories. The first symptom is re-experiencing, which occurs when an individual involuntarily and vividly relives the traumatic event. This may present in the form of flashbacks, nightmares, or recurring distressing thoughts, images, or physical sensations such as trembling, nausea, sweating, or pain. Individuals may also struggle with persistent negative thoughts about the trauma, often questioning why it happened or whether they could have prevented it. These ruminations can lead to feelings of guilt and shame, as individuals may blame themselves for something which was actually never their fault.

The second symptom is avoidance and emotional numbing. This includes efforts to avoid reminders of the trauma, such as specific people, places, or conversations. Individuals may try to suppress memories of the abuse or distract themselves by keeping busy. Some may cope by shutting down emotionally, which can result in social withdrawal and a loss of interest in previously enjoyable activities.

The third symptom is hyperarousal, where individuals feel constantly on edge or alert. This heightened state of anxiety can lead to irritability, sudden outbursts of anger, difficulty sleeping and problems with concentration. People experiencing hyperarousal may be easily startled and feel unable to relax, which can further interfere with daily functioning (NHS, 2022).

- **dissociative identity disorder (DID)**: in severe cases, individuals who have experienced childhood abuse may develop psychiatric conditions, such as *dissociative identity disorder*. DID, formerly referred to as *multiple personality disorder* (MPD), is a mental health condition characterised by the presence of two or more distinct identities or personality states that alternately take control of a person's behaviour. These identities can have their own names, voices, memories and behaviours (Saxena et al., 2023)

  While the disorder may begin in childhood, it is typically diagnosed in adulthood as thorough assessments over extended periods are often necessary for an accurate diagnosis. In certain religious, spiritual and cultural contexts, DID is sometimes interpreted as a form of demonic possession (Mitra and Jain, 2023). Where DID is present, research indicates that dissociative symptoms, including identity alterations, are closely linked to the severity of childhood abuse individuals have experienced. However, it is important to note that not all individuals who endure extreme childhood maltreatment develop dissociative symptoms and, conversely, some individuals with significant dissociative symptoms may not have ever experienced childhood maltreatment (Daniels et al., 2024).

Activity 4.1: MPD to DID

The shift from the term 'multiple personality disorder' to DID represents a significant change in how this condition is understood and diagnosed in the present day. While MPD previously emphasised separate personalities, DID is focused on dissociation, which is recognised as the key feature of the disorder. This shift reflects a deeper understanding of how DID does not involve completely separate personalities, but rather comprises different identity states that emerge as a result of trauma and dissociation. This shift in terminology also illustrates the influence of dominant voices in psychiatry, highlighting the power of language in shaping the way mental health conditions are perceived, diagnosed and treated.

Reflective questions

1. How does labelling conditions in different ways impact on society's perceptions of mental ill health?
2. In what ways does the renaming of psychiatric disorders reflect broader social, political, or cultural influences on mental healthcare?

Long-term impact on adult coping mechanisms

For some, the experience of childhood abuse can disrupt the development of healthy emotional regulation and coping strategies. As victims/survivors of abuse navigate adulthood, some individuals may adopt coping mechanisms aimed at managing unresolved trauma, overwhelming emotions and psychological distress. These strategies can range from adaptive responses to maladaptive behaviours, such as self-harm, eating disorders, or substance misuse, which are outlined below.

Substance misuse: Research suggests that individuals who have experienced child abuse are more likely to turn to substances (alcohol, drugs etc.) as a means of coping with distress (Rakovski et al., 2024). Childhood trauma can contribute to substance use/misuse through both direct and indirect pathways. The direct pathway involves using substances as a form of self-medication to alleviate the emotional pain caused by the trauma. The indirect pathway occurs when trauma leads to substance use as a means of psychological dissociation, helping individuals suppress troubling emotions and sensations (Schimmenti et al., 2022).

Eating disorders: Research on the link between child abuse and eating disorders presents mixed findings, highlighting the complexity of the connection between the two. Caslini et al. (2016) analysed data from over 14,000 individuals and found that bulimia nervosa and binge eating disorder were significantly linked to childhood abuse, whereas anorexia nervosa showed a less clear association. Another study found that emotional abuse was a stronger predictor of eating disorders than physical or sexual abuse, indicating how experiences of shame, low self-worth and a lack of control may contribute to eating disorder behaviours (Kent et al., 1999).

Gender differences may also influence this relationship, as research has shown that men who experience sexual abuse or neglect are at greater risk of developing eating disorders, whereas for women, sexual and emotional abuse are the strongest risk factors (Afifi et al., 2017). Additionally, research shows that women who experienced physical abuse were twice as likely to develop symptoms of an eating disorder, while those who suffered both physical and sexual abuse were three times more likely to be diagnosed with an eating disorder (Rayworth et al., 2004).

Self-harm: Self-harm is defined as the direct and intentional infliction of damage to one's own body tissue, with or without the intention to die, and for purposes not culturally sanctioned (Gratz, 2001). Research shows that the trauma associated with childhood experiences of maltreatment increases the likelihood of individuals engaging in self-harming behaviours as a coping mechanism during childhood or adulthood. Individuals who begin self-harming at a young age are also more likely to continue using this behaviour as a long-term coping strategy (Manus et al., 2019). The emotional distress caused by experiences of abuse can result in a need or desire to escape or numb overwhelming feelings, leading some individuals to use self-harm as a means of exerting control over their feelings and attempting to temporarily relieve psychological suffering (Chapman et al., 2006).

Suicidal ideation and suicide attempts: Although suicidal thoughts can lead to attempted suicide, Klonsky and May (2015) propose that suicidal thoughts (ideation) and actual suicide attempts are separate processes. According to this perspective, suicidal thoughts come from a mixture of psychological pain and hopelessness; the likelihood of moving from suicidal thoughts to actual attempts depends on factors such as personal characteristics and having the practical means to carry out the suicide attempt.

Research evidence indicates that adults who experienced abuse during their childhood are two to three times more likely to have suicidal thoughts and to attempt suicide later in life (Angelakis et al., 2019). Among the different forms of abuse, sexual abuse has been identified as the strongest predictor of suicidal ideation (Bahk et al., 2017), while children who experienced multiple forms of abuse are as much as five times more likely to attempt suicide during adulthood (Angelakis et al., 2019).

Long-term impact on adult physical health

Child abuse can also lead to significant physical health challenges during adulthood. Adult victims/survivors of abuse are understood to be at higher risk of developing chronic physical health conditions such as heart disease, diabetes and autoimmune disorders. This, in part, has been attributed to the long-term stress and trauma associated with the abuse, which can lead to impact on the body's stress response system (Danese and McEwen, 2012). Experiencing traumatic stress during childhood has been shown to significantly increase the risk of hospitalisation for autoimmune diseases in adulthood (Dube et al., 2009). In addition, those who experienced physical abuse are more likely to develop chronic pain conditions later in life, such as fibromyalgia or migraines (Springer et al., 2007). Evidence also suggests that childhood abuse (across all subtypes) is associated with a heightened risk of developing coronary heart disease in adulthood (Chen et al., 2023).

Long-term impact on adult relationships

Adults who experienced abuse as children often see the impact on their relationships; for example, one study found that both male and female victims of abuse had higher rates of separation and divorce compared to the control group. Additionally, abused and neglected females were less likely than their female counterparts to view their current romantic partners positively or to remain sexually faithful (Colman and Widom, 2004). More specifically, in terms of sexual abuse, the damaging impact it can have on the ability to form and maintain loving relationships, both intimate and platonic, is noted. Many individuals who experienced sexual abuse as a child struggle to open up to partners, family and friends about their experiences, which further impacts on their connection with others (IICSA, 2018).

Long-term economic impact on adults

The impact of child abuse can also extend beyond individual mental and physical health consequences and may affect a person's ability to work and achieve economic stability during their lives. Research shows that victims/survivors of abuse are more likely to have lower levels of education, employment, earnings and fewer assets as adults (Currie and Widom, 2010; Zielinski, 2009). These disadvantages are often linked to higher rates of unemployment and reduced earning potential compared to the general population. Such economic challenges can persist over time, limiting opportunities for financial independence and long-term economic security.

The impact of child abuse on wider society

Child abuse is not only an individual adverse childhood experience, but also a significant societal issue with far-reaching consequences. Beyond the immediate harm to victims, its effects ripple through families, public services and economies. Child abuse may lead to intergenerational impact and increased reliance on social support systems. Public services, including healthcare, education, social care and the criminal justice system, also bear significant financial and operational pressures due to the prevalence of child abuse.

Intergenerational transmission of abuse: The intergenerational transmission of abuse refers to when individuals who have experienced abuse go on to behave in similarly abusive ways towards their own children (Thornberry et al., 2012). Understanding the intergenerational transmission of abuse requires caution, as it can be misleading and harmful to assume that all victims/survivors of abuse will go on to perpetrate abuse. However, there is evidence to suggest that child abuse has the potential to be passed down from one generation to the next, particularly in the case of physical abuse. Research shows how individuals who experienced physical abuse during their own childhood are more likely to physically abuse their own children (Pears and Capaldi, 2001); yet although some adult victims/survivors may struggle with parenting appropriately, intergenerational transmission is by no means inevitable (Greene et al., 2020).

Victim-to-perpetrator cycle: The victim-to-perpetrator cycle refers to the idea that some individuals who experience abuse, particularly child sexual abuse (CSA), may later become perpetrators themselves. For example, research suggests that sex offenders are more likely to have a history of CSA compared to non-sex offenders (Jespersen et al., 2009). A study by Glasser et al. (2001) also found a link between CSA and later perpetration, particularly among males. Among the 747 male participants, 35 per cent of perpetrators had been victims themselves. Notably, men abused by a female during childhood were more likely to offend (Glasser et al., 2001; Salter et al., 2003), whereas female victims were significantly less likely to become perpetrators (Glasser et al., 2001). Overall, however, the evidence linking victimisation to later perpetration remains limited (see Chapter 5), and CSA experiences do not inevitably lead to sexual offending in adulthood.

Economic costs: The economic costs of child abuse are substantial, affecting not only individuals but also society as a whole. Research from the UK has identified significant financial impacts on society resulting from child abuse. Research estimates the discounted average lifetime cost of non-fatal child maltreatment by a primary caregiver at £89,390 per victim, with major contributors being social care, short-term healthcare and long-term labour market outcomes. The same study estimated the discounted lifetime cost per death from child maltreatment at £940,758, encompassing healthcare and lost productivity costs (Conti et al., 2021). Additionally, a report by the Home Office, which assessed the economic cost on society for child sexual abuse in England and Wales, estimated this to be at least £10.1 billion over a period of a year (Home Office, 2021).

Public service costs: A 2021 report by the House of Lords Public Services Committee concluded that the UK faces a 'crisis in child vulnerability' with health, social care, education and criminal justice services often stretched due to the increasing demand for child protection interventions. Public services costs are associated with the following:

a. **health**: healthcare expenses include both short- and long-term costs associated with physical and mental health issues. These include treatment for conditions such as depression and PTSD, as well as care for self-inflicted harm. Additional costs arise from emergency services, including ambulance transportation, hospitalisation, emergency and inpatient admissions, interhospital transfers, readmissions, rehabilitation and other medical interventions;
b. **social care**: child welfare service costs include care placements, infant homes, parent support centres and therapeutic facilities for emotionally affected children. This also includes administrative expenses related to child protection agencies and local authority social care services;
c. **education**: costs related to education are based on the increasing demand for special education services and school-based interventions to support children affected by abuse, as well as additional resources required for mental health support and behaviour management within educational settings;
d. **criminal justice**: criminal justice costs refer to the expenses incurred in investigating and prosecuting child abuse cases, including legal aid, court proceedings and the incarceration or rehabilitation of offenders. This also includes the financial cost of victim support programmes within the justice system.

(Conti et al., 2021)

Activity 4.2: Child abuse and the role of public services

Bethany is a 15-year-old girl who has recently been placed in foster care following a prolonged period of neglect and physical abuse at home that began when she was eight. Her placement was made following escalating concerns raised by multiple agencies.

Bethany has been struggling to attend school regularly. Staff have noted her disengagement from learning and frequent absences, and concerns have been raised about her emotional wellbeing. She has been referred to Child and Adolescent Mental Health Services (CAMHS), where she is receiving support for anxiety and low mood.

Bethany's foster placement has become increasingly unstable, as her challenging behaviours have placed considerable strain on her carers. Her allocated social worker continues to work intensively with Bethany and her foster family to offer support.

Bethany has also come into contact with the police due to her association with local teenagers involved in antisocial behaviour. The youth justice service is now aware of her case, and discussions are underway about appropriate next steps.

(Continued)

Reflective questions

Education

- How might Bethany's experiences affect her ability to engage in learning?
- What additional education-based resources may be available to support Bethany?

Health

- What are the potential short- and long-term health consequences for Bethany?
- What additional health interventions could support Bethany's needs?

Social care

- What social care interventions would be required to support Bethany in the immediate and long term?
- How could early intervention have changed Bethany's circumstances?

Criminal justice

- How might Bethany's experiences of abuse and neglect influence her involvement with antisocial behaviour?
- What interventions could the criminal justice system provide to support Bethany?

Summary

This chapter has explored the multifaceted impact of child abuse, highlighting the immediate and long-term consequences for children and adults, and the impact on wider society. At an individual level, children who are subjected to abuse often experience profound physical, psychological and developmental challenges which can affect their wellbeing and relationships. Child abuse can also significantly disrupt children's cognitive development, which in turn may hinder educational achievement. The consequences of abuse are therefore not confined to the period during which it occurs; they often continue to shape an individual's life experiences long after the abuse has ended.

The chapter also explored the potential long-term impact of child abuse on adult victims/survivors, illustrating how adverse early life experiences can contribute to chronic physical and mental health conditions, affect relationships and lead to economic instability in adulthood. Beyond these individual consequences, the chapter examined broader societal implications, such as the intergenerational transmission of abuse and financial strain of child maltreatment on the economy. By emphasising the interplay between individual and societal impact, this discussion demonstrates that child abuse is a pervasive concern rather than solely an individual or family matter. The far-reaching impact of power, channelled through abusive behaviour towards children, reinforces the critical role of social workers in delivering power-informed interventions that address both individual needs and wider concerns.

5

Perpetrators of child abuse

Introduction

Questions around who perpetrators of child abuse are and why they commit such acts have long been subjects of psychological, sociological and criminological inquiry. Research has explored factors such as childhood trauma, social learning and cognitive distortions to understand offending behaviour (Smallbone et al., 2008). However, no single explanation fully accounts for the complexities of child abuse perpetration, as abusive behaviour often stems from an interplay of various factors. For the purposes of exploring the phenomenon, this chapter is divided into three parts to guide social workers from foundational data, through specific theoretical insights, to critical reflection.

Part one of this chapter examines demographic data on who commits child abuse and in what context, drawing in particular on the Crime Survey for England and Wales (CSEW). It also considers the subject of perpetrators of child sexual exploitation and institutional abuse within the UK. Part two then focuses on the subject of child sexual abuse (CSA) and presents psychological and sociological perspectives which attempt to explain the *how* and *why* of CSA, including research perspectives on female CSA offenders. Finally, part three critically examines notions of the *intergenerational transmission of abuse* and *victim to perpetrator* cycle in further detail. As a whole, this chapter aims to deepen social workers' understanding of who perpetrates child abuse, the factors that drive their behaviour and the implications for more informed practice.

Who perpetrates child abuse?

There remain large gaps within the existing global data on both the prevalence and the perpetrators of different forms of violence against children (Devries et al., 2018). Though some world nations may be unable to publicly share, or feel uncomfortable about publicly sharing child abuse-related statistics, the 2015 to 2016 CSEW ran a module of questions, which asked adults about their historic experiences of child abuse. Table 5.1 (based on the data) is a breakdown of the reported perpetrators for different categories of child abuse, drawn from the survey.

Note: Participants could name more than one perpetrator, so figures sum to >100 per cent.

Table 5.1 Reported perpetrators for different categories of child abuse (per cent)

Abuse type	Mum	Dad	Step father	Step mother	Other family	Partner	Friend	Authority figure	Stranger	Other
Psychological	40	35	12	4	14	16	10	5	4	3
Physical	29	39	10	2	10	12	7	5	9	3
Sexual (rape/ penetration)	1	7	8	–	26	8	30	6	14	7
Other sexual assault	1	4	5	–	16	5	23	6	42	7

The data shows that, in cases of psychological abuse, 40 per cent of victims identified their mother and 35 per cent their father as the perpetrator. For physical abuse, fathers were most frequently reported (39 per cent), followed by mothers (29 per cent), with fewer cases involving stepparents and other relatives. Overall, approximately 80 per cent of physically abusive perpetrators were family members.

In contrast, child sexual abuse (CSA) shows a very different pattern. For rape or penetration (including attempts), victims most often reported a friend (30 per cent) or other family member (26 per cent) as the perpetrators rather than parents, who equated to a very small percentage in comparison. For 'other' sexual assaults, non-family perpetrators were most common. The survey found that the largest category of perpetrators were strangers (around 42 per cent), followed by friends (23 per cent). Therefore, well over half of the cases of sexual assault involved non-family offenders.

From the data, it becomes apparent that family perpetrators account for the majority of psychological and physical abuse cases, whereas a much larger proportion of sexual abuse appears to be inflicted by non-family individuals. Mothers and fathers together account for roughly three quarters of childhood emotional and physical abuse, but only a small fraction of sexual assaults by rape/penetration. Strangers are rare as perpetrators of psychological or physical abuse; however, they are the single largest category for 'other' sexual assault.

Alongside the CSEW, other UK-based research such as the NSPCC child maltreatment study (Radford et al., 2011) includes a consideration of the prevalence of CSA committed by children under the age of 18. Of the participants who reported experiencing contact sexual abuse before the age of 18, 57.5 per cent said the perpetrator was another child or young person, 34.1 per cent identified an adult and 8.4 per cent reported abuse by both adults and young people. Additionally, broader research based on secondary data from 171 countries shows that household members are the most common perpetrators of both physical and emotional violence against children of all ages, with prevalence rates often exceeding 50 per cent. Student peers are the next most frequent source of such abuse. Among girls aged 15–19, intimate partners are the most commonly reported perpetrators of sexual violence. Despite these findings, there remains a recognised need for more systematically collected global data on different types of child abuse perpetrators. For example, reliable data on abuse by authority figures, siblings and other adults remains scarce (Devries et al., 2018).

Perpetrators of child sexual exploitation in the UK and ethnicity

A rapid evidence assessment (Walker et al., 2018) synthesised findings from 50 studies examining the characteristics and motivations of CSE perpetrators, most of whom were identified as male, White, aged 30–46 and in employment, often in professional roles. The vast majority of research (37 studies) focused exclusively on online CSE offenders, with very limited data on non-online, group-based or other forms of CSE. Where motivations were explored, sexual gratification and financial gain emerged as primary drivers for CSE perpetrators. Furthermore, a 2020 government report noted that known group-CSE perpetrators are most commonly White, although some studies find marginal over-representation of Black and Asian men relative to their population share (Home Office, 2020a). However, the same report stresses that this evidence base is limited, warning that data quality problems make it impossible to draw firm conclusions. Crucially, it concludes that 'it is likely that no one community or culture is uniquely predisposed to offending' (Home Office, 2020a, p. 25). The Independent Inquiry into Child Sexual Abuse (IICSA, 2022a) likewise found that inconsistent ethnicity recording makes it impossible to know whether any particular ethnic group is over-represented among perpetrators of CSE (ibid.). Similarly, the Casey report (Casey, 2025) emphasises the ongoing lack of reliable data on group-based CSE, particularly in relation to the ethnicity of perpetrators. It highlights how the data held in some local areas showed that men from ethnic minority backgrounds are over-represented as perpetrators in group-based CSE specifically in those areas, but generalisations could not be made as ethnicity data collected for victims and perpetrators of group-based CSE is insufficient to allow any conclusions to be drawn at the national level. Instead, the review recommended that there is a need to, 'revise and improve the collection of ethnicity and nationality data of both suspects and victims for all sexual abuse and exploitation cases' (Casey, 2025, p. 152) in order to build a clearer picture.

In public discourse, claims that CSE gangs are overwhelmingly from minority communities (e.g., 'Muslim grooming gangs' or 'Pakistani grooming gangs') have been widely discredited as sensationalist (Cockbain and Tufail, 2020). Academics note that this narrative is misleading and harmful and point out that the oft-cited figure of 84 per cent Asian heritage offenders (from Rafiq and Adil, 2017, a Quilliam report) is methodologically flawed and unreliable (Cockbain and Tufail, 2020; IICSA, 2022a). In summary, peer-reviewed and official sources agree that most convicted CSE offenders in the UK are White, and there is no robust evidence to support the notion that any ethnic minority group is disproportionately represented once known under-reporting and data gaps are considered. Nevertheless, the upcoming changes in data recording practices in the UK (Public Services Committee Report, 2025) will enable better insights into understanding the link between group-based CSE and ethnicity. Until then, we can only conclude that the overall findings thus far reflect how power operates not only through the actions of perpetrators, but also through flawed data practices and subsequent racialised narratives which are present within public discourse relating to CSE (Muzaffar, 2025).

Power and professionals as perpetrators of institutional abuse in the UK

Seventy inquiries investigating child abuse were identified as having taken place in the UK between 1945 and 1998 (Corby et al., 1998). UK-based inquiries (Frizzell, 2009; Kirkwood, 1993; Marshall et al., 1999; Shaw, 2007; Skinner, 1992) have consistently (either directly or indirectly) acknowledged the role of power among professionals and within institutions in enabling and sustaining abusive behaviours and practices. Although such inquiries were not undertaken on a national level, they demonstrate how investigating child abuse within institutions is not a new or recent phenomenon. This long-standing pattern of localised investigations perhaps laid the groundwork for more comprehensive examinations, ultimately culminating in the establishment of national inquiries in the UK such as the Independent Inquiry into Child Sexual Abuse (IICSA), which sought to investigate institutional failings across England and Wales.

Independent Inquiry into Child Sexual Abuse in England and Wales (IICSA)

Although there are inherent challenges present in evaluating inquiry outcomes (Wright, 2017), IICSA represented a significant national effort to systematically examine institutional responses to CSA across England and Wales, aiming to uncover systemic failings and recommend reforms. Launched in 2015, IICSA was tasked with investigating how institutions fulfilled, or failed to fulfil, their duty to protect children from sexual abuse. This involved examining how professionals and their respective institutions, including care homes, charitable organisations, churches and local authorities, responded to allegations and disclosures of CSA that occurred within settings they managed or were responsible for overseeing. IICSA highlighted various patterns of abuse, with the final report describing offenders who 'groomed victims and befriended parents' to create a 'veneer of genuine affection which … enabled the abuse' (IICSA, 2022b, p. 3). However, some individuals reported that their circumstances made them so vulnerable that grooming was irrelevant because perpetrators had complete power over them and were able to abuse them at will (ibid., p. 41). Throughout the IICSA the issue of power is repeatedly emphasised, not only as central to the abuse itself, but also in shaping the impact – for example:

> *Freddie's abuser was a teacher whose power and influence extended into the church, a business and a sports team in the local area. He feels this network of control made it easier for the man to abuse many young people.*
>
> *A teacher at Diane's school exploited his position of power and authority to sexually abuse her. From then until now, the emotions and effects this caused for her have included feeling flattered, confused, depressed, anxious and suicidal.*
>
> (Truth Project, 2018, pp. 12 and 55)

Many victims/survivors described feeling frightened, powerless and trapped, unable to escape the sexual abuse they endured (IICSA, 2022b, p. 57). In religious settings specifically, individuals noted that the 'power, authority and reverence bestowed upon religious institutions and the individuals working within them meant that the conduct of perpetrators went unquestioned' (ibid., p. 384). Peer-on-peer abuse was also identified as a serious issue, primarily framed within the context of 'harmful sexual behaviour' between children. This form of abuse was often poorly understood and inadequately managed by professionals charged with safeguarding children. However, the IICSA recognised that the majority of perpetrators held professional authority within their institutions. Those in professional roles included care home staff, healthcare practitioners, priests, teachers and others who used their positions of power to exploit and abuse children.

Historical Institutional Abuse Inquiry in Northern Ireland (HIA)

The Northern Ireland Historical Institutional Abuse (HIA) Inquiry investigated the sexual, physical, emotional abuse and neglect of children within care institutions, and examined how state and religious organisations managed, or failed to prevent child abuse (Hart, 2017). The HIA inquiry found similar power dynamics present, as the inquiry documented how abuse was perpetrated by authority figures who were entrusted with children's care.

> *One applicant explained that soon after her admission to the establishment she was 'set aside' by a male member of staff: 'He paid me more attention.' She trusted him and told him about the abuse she had experienced at home, including sexual abuse. He hugged her when she cried and always came to her aid when she asked for him. As he was a senior member of staff she said that he had a great deal of power. This grooming behaviour escalated, progressing from kissing her to full sexual intercourse on a regular basis, from the age of sixteen through to eighteen and beyond, including after she had left the establishment.*
>
> (Ibid., p. 262)

The inquiry documented the profound feelings of powerlessness experienced by children, often exacerbated by the collusion of professionals. This included religious representatives, whose involvement was frequently evident in the concealment of abuse and poor practice within institutions. One victim/survivor recounted, 'Any brother who wanted to abuse us did. The others turned a blind eye and didn't say anything' (ibid., 2017, p. 33). Similarly to the findings of the England and Wales Inquiry, the vast majority of perpetrators identified in the HIA were male. However, nuns and female care staff were also identified as holding positions of authority and were sometimes guilty of either directly perpetrating abuse or failing to intervene when abuse occurred. The issue of peer-on-peer abuse was also raised in relation to some institutions, where inadequate staffing levels hindered the ability to address the problem; and the failure to safeguard children was widespread throughout the system. Overall, the HIA found that perpetrators were predominantly adults who had authority over children, and that their institutional privilege, often protected by cover-ups or inaction, enabled the abuse to continue for many years.

Scottish Child Abuse Inquiry (SCAI)

In Scotland, the Scottish Child Abuse Inquiry (SCAI) began in 2015 and in 2025 remains ongoing. Its remit is to investigate the abuse of children in institutional care settings such as children's homes, foster care, boarding schools and secure units. The inquiry has published a number of case studies and witness testimonies which refer to perpetrators; while the final report is yet to be published, the various case studies identify a number of male perpetrators who abused children. At Gordonstoun boarding school and its junior school Aberlour, for example, the inquiry found that a male physics teacher was a predatory paedophile, who groomed boys with a view to satisfying his sexual desires. Other professionals, including other teachers, a housemaster and a chaplain were also identified as being perpetrators of abuse between the 1960s and 1990s.

The SCAI clearly notes, 'a significant failure of governance with no interest in child protection or pastoral care until the 1990s', suggesting that leaders did not appropriately address abusive behaviour, whereby 'a dreadfully abusive and, in some houses, extremely violent culture was allowed to take root' (SCAI, 2024, n.p.). Findings from the SCAI appear to echo the findings from the other UK-based inquiries, as professional staff often held unchecked power over children and used it to abuse them. Similar to the findings of other inquiries, the Scottish example highlights how institutional authority was one of the key enablers that allowed perpetrators to use their power in ways that victimised children.

Activity 5.1: Institutional abuse and power dynamics

Based on the previous section, which considered perpetrators of child abuse in institutional settings, answer the following reflective questions.

1. How did the imbalance of power between children and adults within institutional settings potentially enable the continuation of abuse and silence the voices of child victims? Consider how authority, control and dependence were manipulated by perpetrators and protected by institutional structures.
2. In what ways may institutional power structures (e.g., religious orders, state bodies, school leadership) have prioritised reputation and self-preservation over the safety and rights of children? Reflect on how systemic inaction or cover-ups were expressions of power that reinforced abuse.

Understanding perpetrators of child sexual abuse

Having explored the broader question of who perpetrates child abuse, the following section focuses specifically on perpetrators of CSA. This targeted focus reflects not only the distinctive dynamics associated with CSA, but also its prominence within child protection policy and safeguarding frameworks. By exploring theories which attempt to explain the *why* behind CSA, this discussion aims to support a more in-depth understanding of the phenomenon.

Why do people sexually abuse children? Psychological vs sociological theories

Psychological theories often highlight the role of internal processes and developmental deficits in individuals who commit CSA. One key focus is on *cognitive distortions*, which are self-serving beliefs that allow individuals to justify, minimise, or normalise abusive behaviour (O Ciardha and Ward, 2013). A cognitive distortion is essentially a biased or irrational way of thinking that leads a person to misinterpret or misunderstand reality. Research shows that those who sexually abuse children tend to hold significantly stronger pro-offending cognitive distortions compared to other types of offenders. For example, one study found that perpetrators of CSA often maintain long-standing distorted beliefs that support and rationalise their actions. In contrast, individuals who sexually assault adults are more likely to attribute their behaviour to external factors or situational pressures related to the specific incident, rather than holding enduring beliefs that justify their actions (Blumenthal et al., 1999).

Attachment theory also provides a significant psychological explanation for why some individuals may sexually abuse children. At its core, attachment theory suggests that early relationships with primary caregivers form the blueprint for how individuals understand intimacy, trust and emotional regulation throughout life (Bowlby, 1988). When these early bonds are insecure, inconsistent or abusive, they can severely disrupt a child's ability to form healthy relationships. Research has shown that individuals who sexually abuse children often report histories of disorganised or insecure attachment, which are associated with higher incidences of personality disorders and cognitive distortions (Garofalo and Bogaerts, 2019). In other words, individuals who grow up in environments marked by neglect, inconsistency, or emotional unavailability may internalise harmful beliefs about relationships and intimacy, which can lead them to behave in abusive ways.

In contrast with psychological theories attempting to explain why people sexually abuse children, *sociological theories* tend to focus more on social structures and contexts. Feminist perspectives on the subject argue that CSA is an extreme manifestation of gendered power imbalances. Subsequently, CSA can be viewed as, 'an expression of male supremacy inherent in patriarchy' (Seymour, 1998, p. 415). According to this perspective, patriarchy creates a social environment where men hold power over women and children, while the social construction of masculinity and male sexual socialisation then offers motivations and norms that can legitimise abuse. In simpler words, this means that CSA can be seen as a result of a society where men are often raised to believe they should be dominant, in control and entitled to have their needs met. This process can, in turn, teach males to view sex as a way to assert power rather than as something based on mutual respect. Together, these beliefs can create attitudes that excuse or even justify abusive behaviour.

According to the feminist perspective, therefore, patriarchal power provides the opportunity, while masculine entitlement supplies the motivation to offend (Seymour, 1998). From a *criminology* perspective, 'opportunity' is made more explicit, as some perspectives suggest that perpetrators of CSA do not necessarily groom children with a view to abuse them. But rather, in many cases they seize the opportunity to offend when situational factors permit (Leclerc and Proulx, 2018). For example, when children are available and unsupervised, opportunistic perpetrators are more likely to act on their impulses. In such moments, the lack of adult supervision removes a key protective barrier, increasing the risk of abuse.

Together, these explanations enhance our understanding of why some individuals may sexually abuse children. The sociological explanations complement the psychological view by showing how broader gender and power dynamics, as well as situational factors (such as opportunity), may interact with a sexual offender's individual distortions and attachment deficits and lead to CSA.

Activity 5.2: Finkelhor (1984) The Four Preconditions model

Consider the following model, which was foundational in understanding CSA as a process involving psychological, social and situational dynamics rather than a purely pathological act, and reflect on the questions which follow.

The Four Preconditions model proposes that four conditions must be present for CSA to occur.

1. The individual must have a motivation to sexually abuse a child.
   The offender's motivation is further explained as involving three key elements:
   a. a degree of emotional congruence with regards to the abusive act with the child;
   b. the capacity to become sexually aroused by the child and the sexual activity;
   c. a sense of being blocked from meeting their emotional or sexual needs in socially acceptable or lawful ways.
2. The individual must be able to overcome internal restraints or inhibitors, such as feelings of guilt, fear or moral opposition.
3. The individual must be able to circumvent external obstacles/inhibitors such as the lack of opportunity or the presence of protective adults.
4. The individual must be able to overcome any resistance from the child, which can involve grooming, manipulation, coercion, or threats.

Reflective questions

1. What insights does the Four Preconditions model offer into the psychological and situational factors that contribute to CSA?
2. In what ways does the model challenge or reinforce common assumptions about perpetrators of CSA?
3. What role might emotional congruence play in shaping an offender's justification for their actions?

Female perpetrators of child sexual abuse

Research and official reports consistently indicate that males constitute the vast majority of perpetrators of CSA. Recent research indicates that male perpetrators make up 91.7 per cent of offenders, with 3.8 per cent being female-only perpetrators (Karsna and Kelly, 2021); another study suggests that females in the general population are responsible for up to 5 per cent of reported child sex offences in the UK (Augarde and Rydon-Grange, 2022). More recently still, a police analysis of CSA and exploitation in England and Wales has found that 82 per cent of recorded crimes of this nature involve male offenders, with a very low percentage of CSA committed by females alone (NPCC, 2024). While female perpetrators represent a much smaller proportion of offenders in comparison to males, their presence is nonetheless a reality that requires recognition and further understanding.

A UK-based research study examined female perpetrators of CSA, whose ages ranged from 21 to 56 years, with a mean age of 31.2. Within the sample the women were typically aged between 26 and 31 years old (45.1 per cent, n = 55) when they first sexually abused a child. In other words, nearly half were in their late 20s to early 30s at onset. Therefore, very few female offenders were teenagers or over 40 years when they first perpetrated sexual abuse (Darling, 2018, p. 142). In the same study, it was found that female perpetrators were more likely to be motivated by the need to fulfil emotional needs or sexual desires rather than for purposes of material gain; 48.8 per cent of female perpetrators were categorised as being motivated by intimacy/emotional needs and 45.1 per cent by sexual gratification (ibid., p. 170).

It is also noted that female perpetrators are more likely to sexually abuse boys than girls (Karsna and Kelly, 2021); typically using emotional manipulation and grooming, rather than overt force, to enable the abuse (Darling, 2018). Research notes that, 'the vast majority of female child sex offenders appear to use persuasion rather than physical violence or force to coerce their victims or prevent disclosure' (ibid., p. 43). Typically, therefore, female offenders attempt to gain a child's trust rather than resort to violence, and tend to groom children into compliance without the use of physical force.

To conclude, while female perpetrators of CSA represent a very small proportion of the overall population of child sex offenders, their actions are no less serious. A lower prevalence does not equate to lesser significance, particularly for the children who are affected. Every instance of abuse warrants recognition, therefore a deeper understanding of female-perpetrated CSA is essential to developing truly inclusive prevention and safeguarding strategies.

Intergenerational transmission of abuse and the victim to perpetrator cycle

Historically, there has been much debate on whether children who experience abuse are likely to become perpetrators themselves as adults. Two related but distinct concepts are often discussed in this context: the *intergenerational transmission of abuse* (Widom et al., 2015), which refers to abuse being passed from one generation to the next, and the *victim to perpetrator cycle* (Glasser et al., 2001), which suggests that experiences of victimisation may influence how individuals later engage in abusive behaviour beyond familial settings. Research in this area highlights that while experiences of childhood maltreatment increase the risk of future abusive behaviour, this pathway is neither inevitable nor always directed towards children. Research evidence reveals nuanced patterns depending on gender, type of abuse and later life circumstances, some of which is summarised below.

Widom's (1989) study provided prospective evidence that childhood abuse and neglect significantly increase the risk of violent offending in adulthood. However, this violent behaviour was more commonly directed towards adults rather than children. The study found that individuals who had experienced physical abuse or neglect were 38 per cent more likely to be arrested for a violent crime compared to those without such histories. While physical abuse was most strongly linked to later violent behaviour, neglect was associated with broader patterns of antisocial conduct. However, CSA did not show a significant independent link to later violence in this study. Gender differences were also evident, with males more likely than females to be arrested for violent crimes. Importantly, not all abused or neglected children went on to commit violence, highlighting the role of protective factors and the potential for early intervention to prevent this cycle.

Glasser et al. (2001) examined the victim to perpetrator cycle in terms of CSA in the UK, which involved analysing the clinical case notes of 843 individuals attending a specialist forensic psychotherapy centre. The study found that, among the 747 male participants, there was a positive correlation between having experienced CSA and later becoming a perpetrator of CSA, with 35 per cent of male perpetrators reporting that they had been victims themselves. In contrast, among the 96 female participants, although 43 per cent had experienced sexual abuse, only one had gone on to perpetrate CSA. The findings suggest that a victim to perpetrator cycle existed for a subset of male offenders, but did not appear to apply to the female victims in the study. The data therefore suggests some pattern of abuse transmission for male sex offenders, but does not suggest an inevitability, as the majority of male victims did not become perpetrators and female victims almost never did.

Dixon et al. (2005) undertook a study which analysed data from health visits for newborns, which included 4,351 families. As part of the research they compared 135 families in which at least one parent reported childhood abuse (abused-parent (AP) families) with a matched group of non-abused-parent (NAP) families and found that, within the first 13 months after birth, 6.7 per cent of families with a history of childhood abuse experiences were referred for concerns about maltreating their own child, compared to 0.4 per cent of families with no such history. Thus, even among the 'high-risk' group (parents who were abused), well over 90 per cent did not go on to abuse their children. Further analysis showed that the combination of poor parenting styles and three specific risk factors – becoming a parent before age 21, having a history of mental illness or depression and living with a violent partner – explained 62 per cent of the likelihood that childhood abuse would lead to future maltreatment. In other words, a history of abuse raised the risk of later perpetration only when combined with other stressors in the majority of cases. In a related study, it was found that some parents with histories of childhood abuse do not go on to maltreat their own children, with protective factors such as financial stability, strong social support and access to resources helping to break the cycle of abuse (Dixon et al., 2008).

Madigan et al. (2019) undertook an extensive review of 142 research studies on the intergenerational transmission of abuse. These studies were reviewed for how rigorously they were undertaken and also analysed for the different types of abuse they considered. The results showed a moderate link between parents being abused as children and later abusing their own children. The connection was strongest for emotional abuse, followed by physical abuse, sexual abuse and neglect. They also found that the better the quality of the study, the weaker the link appeared, especially for physical abuse. So, overall, this review supports the notion that abuse can be passed down from one generation to the next, but the connection is not very strong, and most people who were abused as children do not go on to abuse others.

In summary, research consistently shows that the majority of individuals who experience child abuse do not go on to abuse others. A history of abuse is therefore not, in itself, a reliable predictor of future perpetration. It is essential for social workers to recognise that while certain risk factors may increase vulnerability, they do not determine a person's future. While some perpetrators do have histories of childhood abuse, a range of moderating factors play decisive roles in breaking any cycles; recognising this complexity can help shift the focus from stigmatising victims/survivors to understanding the multifactorial roots of abusive behaviour.

Activity 5.3: From adversity to reclaiming power

Despite the profound impact of abuse, many victims/survivors transform their adverse experiences into positive actions that benefit themselves and others. This phenomenon, often described as *post-traumatic growth* (Tedeschi and Calhoun, 1996), offers one way of illustrating how individuals can harness their experiences for positive action. For example, one survivor shared: 'The journey to healing is rarely linear, but there is such power and beauty in reclaiming your worth and finding your strength in your own way.' And another survivor, offers support in saying, 'No matter what it is or was, abuse is abuse but please remember it was never your fault. You never deserved it. And you have the power to take back what is rightfully yours' (The Survivors Trust, 2025).

Reflective questions

1. How can experiences of trauma and adversity become sources of strength or motivation for individuals to support others or advocate for change?
2. In what ways does the concept of post-traumatic growth challenge traditional deficit-based views surrounding victims/survivors of abuse?

Summary

Perpetrators of child abuse represent a deeply troubling and complex aspect of human behaviour. Their actions reveal how power and control can be misused to abuse those who are more vulnerable. Understanding why perpetrators perpetrate child abuse requires social workers to look beyond the surface and consider the personal, social and environmental factors which contribute to these harmful behaviours. This chapter, which is by no means exhaustive in its coverage of the subject, has attempted to begin this process of critical thinking on some of the core questions behind the who and why of child abuse. The first part of the chapter considered demographic data which is available from England and Wales, which reveals that mothers and fathers account for the majority of reported psychological and physical abuse, whereas friends, strangers and other non-family figures are responsible for the majority of sexual assaults on children. In relation to child sexual exploitation (CSE) in the UK, official reports and research consistently show that the majority of offenders are male and White, with no evidence to suggest that particular ethnic minority groups are over-represented in the CSE perpetrator demographic nationally. And finally, when considering historic institutional abuse, it becomes apparent that the majority of perpetrators were professional adults who held power and authority over children.

The second part of the chapter explored the complex motivations and contributing factors behind child sexual abuse (CSA), with a focus on both psychological and sociological explanations. Psychological theories emphasise internal processes such as cognitive distortions and attachment deficits, which may lead individuals to justify or normalise abusive behaviour. In contrast, sociological theories highlight the influence of broader social structures, including gendered power dynamics and situational opportunities, in shaping abusive actions. The concluding part of this chapter then went on to unpick ideas around the intergenerational transmission of abuse and the victim to perpetrator cycle. Prospective and retrospective studies confirm that although maltreatment history can raise the risk of later offending, especially when combined with other stressors, the majority of victims/survivors do *not* perpetrate any form of abuse during their lives. This truth challenges simplistic narratives and urges us to see perpetrators not as inevitable products of their pasts, but as individuals whose choices, circumstances and accountability demands a nuanced understanding. Only by confronting the complexity behind these painful realities can social workers foster meaningful intervention to prevent further harm from occurring, to past victims and future children.

6

Revisiting power and power frameworks

Introduction

The preceding chapters explored a range of topics relating to the phenomenon of child abuse, from global perspectives to the subject of perpetrators, consistently highlighting the significance of power. This chapter turns to examine the concept of power itself, with a view to deepening the theoretical understanding that underpins earlier discussions of child abuse, and to lay the groundwork for the practice-focused chapters that follow. The chapter begins by tracing the historical relationship between sociological and social work theory and explores the critical role of power within both, including their influence on current understandings of power which are related to notions of anti-discriminatory practice and empowerment. Following this, a number of frameworks which aim to help social workers navigate power in social work practice are considered and their limitations are highlighted.

To address the gaps in current understandings of power within social work theory and practice, the chapter considers the power-informed practice (PIP) framework (Karim, 2023), which defines power as a dynamic relational force expressed through both action and inaction and categorises its impacts as limiting, productive, or simultaneously both.

Crucially, it also situates the exercise of power on three interconnected levels: the individual/personal (I), professional/institutional (P) and structural/societal (S). The chapter emphasises that understanding power is a professional imperative for social workers and is essential for advancing practice that genuinely empowers individuals and communities.

Sociology, social work and power

Historically, the relationship between sociology and social work has been complex, where disciplinary boundaries have been defined and blurred (Shaw, 2021). It has been recognised that as contemporary social theory increasingly places more emphasis on the individual, it risks overlooking the equally important social and structural influences on people's experiences. It is therefore suggested that sociologists and social workers need to increase their collaborative efforts to become better equipped to address current social challenges (Levin et al., 2015). For this reason, there is a need to revisit the theories and concepts that connect the two disciplines, rather than focus on what separates them – perhaps most significantly, those concerning the subject of power.

The subject of power remains important in both contemporary sociology and social work (Avelino, 2021). In social work, power is often explored through concepts such as empowerment and anti-oppressive practice (Adams, 2008; BASW, 2021; Thompson, 2016). Similarly, power is a key concept in sociology, generating extensive academic debate and diverse interpretations as there is no clear consensus on what power is or how it operates (Haugaard, 2010). Social work practice, which endeavours to be mindful of power, is therefore located among competing and conflicting definitions, highlighting the need for social work practitioners to be clearer in terms of what is understood by power in order to advance practice (Tew, 2006). Nevertheless, differences remain in how power is conceptualised and understood among theorists, therefore the question which is raised is one of validity: which understanding of power is the right understanding of power?

Historic understandings of power as being something concentrated have been replaced with modern day understandings of power as diffuse (Gaventa, 2003). Power debates within academic discourse are recognised to stem from two different perspectives: one focused on domination or *power over* and the other on empowerment or *power to* (Tew, 2002). These perspectives offer valuable insights, yet they also reflect the complexity and contested nature of power as a concept. By drawing on sociological and social work debates and theoretical developments on the subject of power, the process of defining and recognising power within social work practice can truly begin.

Activity 6.1: Defining and recognising power

In attempting to define power, Morriss (2002, p. 1) observes, 'we are all sure we meant something by the word ... but this understanding tends to fade away upon examination'. Take a moment to consider what your understanding of 'power' is.

Reflective questions

1. How would you define power?
2. What power do you think/feel you have and in what context?
3. Where do you see power being exercised in wider society?

It has long been recognised that 'Power … is a universal phenomenon in human societies and in all social relationships' (Bierstedt, 1950, p. 730). Power, therefore, permeates every aspect of human life and is central to the human experience. Recognising the breadth of its reach, as well as how its meaning is shaped by different political and theoretical interests (Lukes, 1986) helps to explain why reaching a shared understanding of power remains an ongoing challenge. As a result, the context in which power is being examined becomes important to consider, as: 'the better definition is the one that accomplishes the task the theorists set for themselves … usefulness is our criterion of evaluation, not some essence lying at the heart of a singular entity' (Haugaard, 2010, p. 426).

Consequently, 'grand' theories of power are increasingly being reconsidered in favour of more nuanced understandings that are grounded in specific contexts. In this way, broader sociological theories of power have informed the thinking of social work theorists such as Tew (2002), Smith (2008) and Dominelli (2002b), whose work offers specific frameworks for analysing power dynamics within the field of social work.

Why is understanding power important in social work?

Both social work theory and practice frameworks emphasise the importance of understanding power dynamics that exist within society (see, for example, Adams, 2008; Dominelli, 2002b; Smith, 2008). Power is recognised as operating at both the micro and macro levels in social relationships (Fook, 2012). In line with this recognition, the social work profession also functions across diverse domains and includes both micro and macro practices, enabling it to effect change on multiple levels (Bent-Goodley, 2014). Efforts to encourage social workers to connect individual practice with broader structural considerations have been ongoing for some time (Bailey and Brake, 1975; Corrigan and Leonard, 1978), reflecting the importance of critically engaging with power across all levels.

Understanding power is therefore essential not only at a structural level, but also in the everyday interactions between social workers and service users. It has been argued that social workers must recognise power not only in terms of their capacity to act, but also in how it is exerted through assumptions and beliefs about individuals (Pullen-Sansfaçon and Cowden, 2012) – assumptions that may themselves be shaped by wider social and structural forces. Power dynamics are understood to hinge on the interplay between social workers' identities, their professional authority and the individuals with whom they engage (Smith, 2008). Therefore, due to their role and professional positioning, social workers exert significant influence through their interactions with service users, with power playing a central role in shaping these dynamics. Consequently, understanding power is essential for ethical and effective social work, as power shapes practice at all levels.

Activity 6.2: Exploring the impact of micro and macro practices in social work

1. **Personal reflection**

   Take a few minutes to reflect on your understanding of the power associated with the social work profession. Consider how the social work profession includes both micro and macro practices, allowing it to effect change on multiple levels.

2. **Discuss or reflect**

   Discuss or reflect on a specific example of when you have observed micro-level social work practices (such as individual or family interventions) alongside macro-level approaches (like community organising, advocacy, or policy development) addressing the same issue.

3. **Analyse and critically reflect**

   Based on your selected example, reflect on the challenges and opportunities present in addressing the issue at different levels. Consider how the integration of micro and macro practices may enhance the effectiveness of social work interventions.

What is power from a social work perspective?

Recognising the importance of power differs considerably from understanding what power actually is and how it operates. Challenges remain in understanding what power is which stem from the broad nature of definitions – the term being value laden, with limitations in the English language and a perceived preoccupation with measuring power rather than understanding its meaning (Bar-on, 2002). Nevertheless, social work has a key role in articulating power relations, identifying their contradictory dynamics and proposing more egalitarian solutions, rooted in principles of social justice (Smith, 2010).

Power remains a contested concept within the field of social work (Dalrymple and Burke, 2006) and, subsequently, power is understood as a multifaceted and diffuse phenomenon (Smith, 2008). The concept of power has been explored on various levels, where power is used to oppress and discriminate against individuals and communities (Thompson, 2016). However, the exercise of power is not exclusively viewed as something negative or limiting; positive and productive expressions of power are also captured within social work theory (Adams, 2008; Tew, 2002), particularly in relation to notions of empowerment and anti-oppressive practice.

How does power relate to empowerment and anti-oppressive practice?

Anti-oppressive practice and empowerment go hand in hand, as empowerment is both a central aim and a practical approach within anti-oppressive social work (Dominelli, 2002b). Given social work's intrinsic association with addressing inequality, the profession is often simultaneously concerned with power, empowerment and anti-oppressive practice (see, for example, Allegri et al., 2022). However, despite their intent, both empowerment and anti-oppressive practice are subject to critique, particularly in how they may inadvertently reproduce the very power imbalances they aim to challenge.

While empowerment is often framed positively, it has also been critiqued as a commodity relationship (Dominelli, 2002a) and the notion of the 'disempowering experience of empowerment' has also been recognised (Fook, 2012, p. 63). Similarly, critiques of anti-oppressive practice highlight a tension between its emancipatory aims and the potential for appropriation, particularly when service users are not meaningfully involved in shaping practice (Wilson and Beresford, 2000). This tension becomes especially apparent in the practical realities of social work, where structural factors and professional roles can inadvertently undermine empowerment.

For example, the requirement for social workers to assess individual needs implies a state of deficit, which may constitute a subtle form of disempowerment from the outset. Moreover, because social work inherently involves both care and control (Dominelli, 2002b), ambiguities persist within its agenda (Parton, 1998). One such ambiguity is evident in decision-making processes about who receives assistance and under what conditions, decisions that are not neutral but shaped by broader power relations. Such processes can therefore reinforce dominant ideas about who is deemed deserving or undeserving of support (Dominelli, 2002b), thereby reinforcing unequal power relations.

It is understandable that thinking about power does not always sit easily with practitioners. On a practice level, social workers may feel uncomfortable with the repressive aspects of their role, particularly when intervening in the lives of individuals. The exercise of power as part of the social work role can also therefore be ambiguous, and this ambiguity may foster a sense of antipathy towards the concept (Karim, 2023). Nevertheless, such conflicted feelings accentuate the need for social workers to develop a deeper understanding of power, its significance and practical application (Bar-On, 2002), in order to effectively navigate the complex power relations present in society (Leonardsen, 2007). To support this, a number of conceptual frameworks have been developed to help practitioners critically engage with power in social work contexts. The following offers a summary of some of these frameworks.

Power frameworks within social work

- **Multi-dimensional model of power**

  Dominelli (2002b) introduced a framework to examine power and its multilayered impact on individuals. The framework identifies various domains, including the client, family, community, national society and the international sphere where power operates – with the physical, psychosocial, economic and spiritual all being noted to create influence. The importance of addressing power relations through anti-oppressive practice to enable the self-empowerment of individuals is also emphasised. However, a key limitation of the model is its complexity, which may impede its effective implementation in practical settings.

- **Model of the child in the world**

  Smith (2004) offers a framework to examine the forces (power) which impact upon children, suggesting that the family, community, state and global context all influence the experiences of a child and that economic forces, social trends, political interests and cultural/religious factors also influence experiences. However, the fact that the framework is based on children's experiences means that its wider application within social work practice is not possible.

- **PCS model**

  Thompson's (2016) PCS model proposes that oppression and discrimination operate on three interconnected levels: the personal or psychological (P), the cultural (C) and the structural (S). The personal level involves individual attitudes and behaviours; the cultural level reflects shared norms and values that perpetuate inequality; and the structural level encompasses institutional and systemic factors. The model emphasises that meaningful and lasting change requires addressing oppression and discrimination across all three levels. The simplicity of the framework allows for a relatively straightforward understanding of the spaces in which power can be used for limiting purposes. However, due to its focus on oppression and discrimination, the model does not readily align with considerations of the more productive and positive manifestations of power.

- **Matrix of power relations**

  The framework offered by Tew (2006) articulates the potential positive and negative exercises of power, as well as the difference in power relations when power is either individually or collectively exercised. Equal consideration of both negative (limiting) and positive (productive) forms of power is a particular strength of the framework as it encourages practitioners not only to challenge harmful or oppressive power dynamics, but also to actively exercise power in productive ways to respond to issues. However, the framework does not capture the duality of impact in the simultaneously positive/negative expressions of power.

Together, these frameworks provide diverse and valuable lenses for understanding and engaging with power in social work practice. While each has its strengths, ranging from highlighting structural oppression to recognising the potential for positive power, they also present limitations that reflect the complexity of applying theoretical models in real-world contexts. To address the limitations identified in existing conceptualisations of power within social work theory, the power-informed practice (PIP) framework was introduced (Karim, 2023). The framework is based on empirical research and builds on existing social work and sociological theory with a view to providing social workers with a tool to understand and work with power within all areas of their practice.

The Power-informed Practice Framework (PiP)

I	Limiting	Limiting/Productive	Productive	I
P	Limiting	Limiting/Productive	Productive	P
S	Limiting	Limiting/Productive	Productive	S

Figure 6.1 The power-informed practice framework (PIP)

Source: Karim, 2023

What is power?

To begin with, let us define what power actually is. Within the framework, power is conceptualised as a dynamic relational force which manifests through both action (to do) and inaction (to not do). Such action or inaction may relate directly or indirectly to human behaviour. Directly power is expressed through observable forms of human action and inaction, while indirectly power is expressed through mechanisms, systems, structures or processes.

How does power impact?

According to the PIP framework, power can impact in limiting, productive and simultaneously limiting/productive ways. The limiting impact of power is aligned with previous understandings of how power can be used in negative, harmful or oppressive ways, while productive power refers to the use of power which impacts in beneficial, empowering or positive ways (see previous discussion on power frameworks). And, finally, the limiting/productive impact of power recognises the duality present in so many expressions of power where both harm (the negative) and benefit (the positive) can be seen – capturing the duality of impact in a new way within social work theory.

Which level is power being exercised on?

The I, P and S levels of the framework help us to recognise which level power is being exercised on, thereby allowing us to determine if the action or inaction is taking place on an individual/personal (I), professional/institutional (P) or structural/societal level (S). These categorisations play a significant role in helping us to understand the scale and form of the power being exercised. The individual/personal level (I) denotes the specific manifestations of power at a micro level, accessible to every individual who has the freedom and ability to make choices, albeit within certain limitations. The professional/institutional (P) mezzo level refers to the power wielded by professionals and institutions, derived from the authority granted to them by the state or community. Lastly, the structural/societal (S) level represents power exercised on a macro scale, through mechanisms which may have potential ramifications for society at large.

How is power exercised at the individual, professional and structural levels?

The individual/personal level (I) within the framework refers to power at a micro level, where individuals have the capacity to exercise power. Such power is accessible to every individual who possesses freedom and the ability to make choices, even if these choices are limited or fall within certain constraints. The term 'individual' is used interchangeably with the 'personal' at this level, emphasising the intricate connection between the two. Personal power is not solely derived from social and contextual factors that provide individuals with greater resources and control, though such factors can significantly enhance it. Personality variables, such as dominant personality traits, also play a crucial role in influencing how individuals experience their sense of power (Anderson et al., 2012).

From a sociological perspective, one of the most significant insights into the exercise of individual power comes from Foucault (1982), who argued that power can emerge from the infinitesimal and is embedded within everyday interactions. Traditional definitions of individual power often revolve around the ability of one entity (A) to influence another (B), as articulated by Dahl (1957, p. 202), or the capacity to control resources, both personal and those which belong to others (Galinsky et al., 2003, p. 454). In similar ways, within the framework, individual/personal power refers to both influence and autonomy. Consequently, this conceptualisation recognises that individuals inherently hold a degree of personal power, which they can actively exercise in various capacities, whether in relation to themselves or others, depending on the specific context in which they find themselves. This acknowledgement emphasises the autonomy and influence that individuals wield at the personal level within the broader PIP framework.

Research summary: Individual power and choice

A study by Inesi et al. (2011) found that both power and choice stem from a fundamental human need for control. Their research showed that when individuals lack power, they often seek choice as a substitute, and vice versa, suggesting that power and choice are psychologically interchangeable, each capable of satisfying the same underlying need. Building on this, Lammers et al. (2016) argue that the desire for autonomy is stronger than the desire to influence others. In their view, the pursuit of power is primarily a quest for control, whether over oneself or one's environment. These insights highlight the importance of examining how individuals use power, particularly in social work practice, where micro-level dynamics shape relationships and outcomes. Understanding the psychological roots of power can help practitioners navigate complex interpersonal situations with greater awareness.

Activity 6.3: Leo's journey, part 1 – individual power

Leo is 15 years old and lives in a disadvantaged neighbourhood in London, which is characterised by poverty, crime and limited opportunities. Growing up, Leo possessed a strong sense of personal power and thought he would set his own path in life and shape his own destiny despite the environment he was living in. However, as Leo reached adolescence, he gave up hope of having a better future when he was sexually abused by a distant relative who visited the family from time to time. Leo tried to tell his elder brother about the abuse, but he didn't believe him. Feeling powerless, Leo began spending more time away from home and gravitated towards a group of older boys, seeking a sense of protection and belonging within the community. Leo found it difficult to cope with the intrusive thoughts he had about the abuse, which led to Leo experimenting with drugs and developing an addiction which he struggled to control. In order to sustain his drug use, Leo occasionally assisted some of the older boys involved in drug dealing. Leo came to terms with his involvement, rationalising it as essential to his survival because it provided both physical protection and a regular source of income.

Reflective question

1. Where is individual power being referred to within the case study and what is the impact of this power?

The professional/institutional (P) level within the framework refers to power at the meso level, where power may be exercised by professionals and institutions based on the authority which has been conferred to them by the state or community. The term 'professional' is used alongside the term 'institutional' to highlight how these two concepts are linked to the exercise of power at the P level within the framework. This is based on the understanding that institutions do not create themselves, nor as a physical structure (if we see them as such) do they autonomously and unilaterally wield power. Instead, it is only by virtue of their professional status that they contain within them particular practices that have been sanctioned. On this level, therefore, the professional and institutional have been brought together to illustrate how professionals and their respective institutions are able to exercise power in line with their status. As a result, whether the power is used by a single professional, or collectively by many, or is the result of the systems which have been created within institutions, power in this context remains professional power.

Weber's (1947) work on power and authority offers valuable insights into understanding the functioning of bureaucracies and the management of institutions, with professionals holding power and institutions reinforcing opportunities for the expression of such power. According to Weber, there are three pure types of legitimate authority, based on rational, traditional and charismatic grounds. Regardless of the type of authority being obeyed, Weber argued that the willingness to comply is based on a belief in the prestige lent to authority figures. Weber further developed the concept of bureaucracy, viewing it as a disciplined system of authority grounded in rational-legal legitimacy. He asserted that for the most stable bureaucratic systems, rational-legal authority was required, which hinges on a belief in the legality of established rules and the authority of those elevated to issue commands (ibid.).

Resonating with Weber's conception of power and authority, the PIP framework defines the professional exercise of power as something which exceeds what is typically accessible to individuals or groups in everyday contexts. Unlike individual-level power, professional power is conferred through additional recognition and is grounded in perceptions of legitimacy and entitlement associated with certain roles. Additionally, within the framework, it is also recognised that professional/institutional power can be sanctioned through both formal and informal mechanisms and systems of authority. Formally, such power is conferred to established organisations and the professionals associated with them, while informally it can be granted to people and settings where power may be exercised outside traditional institutional structures. For example, elders' councils or informal dispute resolution mechanisms may wield considerable influence within communities, despite lacking formal legal status. The PIP framework encourages social work practitioners to critically engage with both dimensions of professional/institutional power, formal and informal, recognising how formal institutional authority intersects with community-based systems which exercise power.

Activity 6.4: Leo's journey, part 2 – professional power

The city of London is experiencing a rise in drug-related crime, leading to growing public dissatisfaction with the police. In response, the police implement a strategy of increased patrols and stop and search measures aimed at curbing drug-related crime and restoring public confidence. During one such patrol, two

(Continued)

officers encounter Leo and his friends hanging around in a park and decide to stop them and carry out a search.

Wanting to hide how afraid he is, Leo becomes confrontational and swears at one of the officers. The officer attempts to arrest Leo, prompting Leo to lash out and push the officer away. In response, both officers use excessive force to throw Leo to the ground and restrain him, which results in Leo being injured before being taken into custody. Despite Leo's repeated requests for medical attention, Leo is arrested on charges of resisting the stop and search and assaulting an officer. He is later released following an initial interview at the police station and taken to hospital, where his injury is treated. While attending hospital for the day, Leo is referred by staff to a drug rehabilitation service, which he agrees to engage with.

Reflective question

1. Where is professional power being referred to within the case study and what is the impact of this power?

The structural/societal (S) level within the framework refers to power at a macro level, where power may be exercised through mechanisms which can impact society at large. For example, power channelled through the law, policy and the media is understood to operate at the structural/societal level. The societal and structural are brought together within the framework as they refer to the power exercised in ways that potentially impact on the whole of society, or at the very least on groups within society. The exercise of such power can be attributed to broad social and structural mechanisms which have the potential to affect the experiences of many, if not all individuals (albeit with varying degrees and forms of impact).

At the structural level within the PIP framework, the work of Giddens (1984) is particularly useful in aiding an understanding of how structural power is exercised and experienced. In a similar way to institutions, social structures are not considered to be independent, objective standalone entities which are devoid of human influence. According to Giddens (ibid.), a dialectic of control exists in social systems whereby both relations of autonomy and dependence exist in social interactions, suggesting a *duality of structure* whereby agency and structure are interdependent. Put simply, this means that people shape society, but are simultaneously restricted by it. Systems, according to Giddens, are the activities of individuals and patterns of social relations, while structures are the rules and resources available to individuals which recreate systems, including for example the likes of class.

Structures are therefore the means and the result; they make action possible, but are also, in effect, the outcome of the action. Essentially, *structuration* refers to the ongoing process through which social systems are produced and reproduced by individuals who draw upon structural rules and resources as they act. According to Giddens (ibid.), structures are both enabling and constraining – that is, they provide the conditions for action while also setting its limits, shaping how power is exercised in social contexts. Reflecting these notions, the exercise of power at the structural/societal (S) level within the PIP framework also refers to the overarching social arrangements present within society, such as cultural norms and social attitudes.

Activity 6.5: Leo's journey, part 3 – structural power

Leo's brother learns of the incident with the police and decides to expose what he perceives to be racialised behaviour through social media. His efforts catch the attention of news reporters, who are actively investigating systemic issues within the UK policing system. Following interviews with Leo and his brother, the news story is released on the mainstream media, which results in a public outcry. Civil rights organisations demand an investigation and support Leo and his family to file a lawsuit against the police department, alleging excessive use of force, unwarranted arrest and a violation of Leo's civil rights. The trial reveals that there has been a pattern of misconduct within the police, including previous allegations around the use of excessive force and a culture of impunity. Following a lengthy trial, the jury finds the officer in question liable for Leo's injury and awards him a substantial amount of money in damages. Additionally, the national government initiates reforms to enhance police transparency and strengthen institutional accountability within police forces across the country.

Reflective question

1. Where is structural power being referred to within the case study and what is the impact of this power?

How can power influence power?

Understanding power requires not only acknowledging the distinct levels at which it is exercised, but also recognising how power exercised at different times and across different levels can be interconnected. Power is not static; its expression in one context can shape or reinforce its expression in another, either immediately or in the long term. Figure 6.2 shows additions to the original diagram aiming to illustrate how these expressions of power can be interconnected according to the PIP framework.

I	Limiting	Limiting/Productive	Productive	I
P	Limiting	Limiting/Productive	Productive	P
S	Limiting	Limiting/Productive	Productive	S

Figure 6.2 The interconnected nature of expressions of power

With nine domains present within the PIP framework, there are countless ways in which expressions of power can influence one another. In some cases, it may be possible to demonstrate (given a relevant case scenario) the existence of a chain of influence, where expressions of power are shaped by previous experiences and continue to evolve throughout an individual's life. This is because, according to the framework, the exercise and impact of power are not confined to a fixed point in time. When power is exerted in one domain and causally impacts another, only for that second domain to reciprocally affect the first, the interplay of power becomes increasingly complex. Also, the point at which we begin our analysis of the power process can significantly shape our understanding of how power is operating, highlighting the importance of perspective in interpreting these dynamics.

Activity 6.6: Leo's journey – the intersections of power

Leo's experiences in parts 1–3 of the case study help us to understand the different levels at which power can operate and how it can impact. According to the PIP framework, power is not static, but a dynamic, relational force that can intersect across the individual, professional and structural levels. Throughout the case study, multiple expressions of power and their interconnectedness at different levels is evident. Based on this understanding, revisit the case study in its entirety and consider the following.

Reflective questions

1. Where in Leo's journey can we see the interaction of different expressions of power?
2. Where in Leo's experiences do past exercises of power affect the present?
3. Where do Leo's experiences of power start, according to the case study, and where do they end?

Summary

This chapter has explored the complex and multifaceted nature of power within social work practice, grounding its discussion in both sociological and social work theory. It also highlighted the contested nature of power, while emphasising the absence of a single, universally agreed-upon definition. The chapter discussed the importance of power in social work, particularly in relation to empowerment and anti-oppressive practice, while recognising the challenges practitioners may face in managing the ambiguous nature of the social work role. These reflections emphasised the need to engage with frameworks that seek to support practitioners in developing a deeper understanding of power within social work practice.

Building on this foundation, the chapter briefly reviewed existing social work frameworks designed to help practitioners critically engage with power and highlighted their limitations, before introducing the power-informed practice (PIP) framework as a contemporary lens for understanding power in social work contexts. To address gaps in existing theory and practice, the framework is used to explain how power is expressed through action and inaction and operates on three interconnected levels: individual/personal (I), professional/institutional (P) and structural/societal (S). The framework also suggests that power can impact individuals in limiting, productive and simultaneously limiting/productive ways. The discussion concluded by reflecting on the intersecting nature of power, highlighting the importance of recognising how past exercises of power can influence present and future experiences. It also explored how power can move across domains, creating a chain of influence that evolves over time. For social workers, this understanding reinforces the need to continually examine how power operates across the individual, professional and structural levels, and adopt a power-informed approach to practice.

7

Power-informed practice for social work

Introduction

Power is at the heart of social work, shaping interactions, influencing decision-making and determining the very structure of service provision. Whether explicitly acknowledged or not, power determines access to resources and affects how individuals and communities experience social work interventions. This chapter expands on the power-informed practice (PIP) framework introduced in the previous chapter (Karim, 2023), with a view to supporting social workers to understand and engage with power in transformative ways in practice.

The chapter begins by examining how the subject of power is addressed in the Independent Review of Children's Social Care (2022b), particularly in its emphasis on the need to shift power within the system. It then introduces the five core principles of PIP, demonstrating how power is contextual and relational, operates across multiple levels, is realised through both action and inaction, has positive, negative, or dual impacts, and is influenced by past experiences. These principles provide a foundation for social workers to critically engage with power, so that it can be exercised reflexively. Drawing on these insights, a three-dimensional model, which operationalises power-informed principles for practice is introduced. This approach distils the complex dynamics of power across three core practice domains: relationships, assessments and interventions.

The chapter then moves on to explore how the integration of PIP principles may enhance existing social work approaches, including the ecological systems, strengths-based, person-centred, trauma-informed and relationship-based practice approaches. Finally, the chapter addresses the limits of professional power, the role of intersectionality and the importance of power-informed supervision. Whether applied as a standalone framework or integrated into existing social work approaches, the chapter demonstrates how the PIP perspective can offer a valuable lens for engaging with power in social work practice.

Power in policy: shaping systems, services and social work

In May 2022, the final report from the Independent Review of Children's Social Care was published (MacAlister, 2022). The report refers to the subject of power throughout and also offers recommendations which may help with the 'reset' of children's social care services. Some of the key messages around power contained within the report include:

1. **Child participation and empowerment**: 'It is paramount that children have a powerful voice in the decisions that affect them' (p. 24*)*. The report refers to the importance of ensuring that children's voices are heard and that they have a degree of influence over decisions affecting their lives. The approach aims to make the system more responsive to both the needs and rights of children.
2. **Empowering local authorities**: 'Decisions about how nationally set objectives are implemented should happen as close to communities and families as possible. This means focusing money, attention and power as close to families and their communities as possible' (p. 39). The report recommends empowering local authorities and partners to lead children's social care, while ensuring that families and communities are actively involved in shaping how services are designed and delivered.
3. **Empowering the workforce**: 'Empower a highly skilled and knowledgeable workforce to create change with children and families' (p. 41). The report emphasises the need for social work practitioners to be equipped with the right skills, resources and support, because an empowered workforce is viewed as essential for high-quality service delivery.
4. **Harnessing the power of communities**: 'Family Help should harness the power of community' (p. 63). The report calls for a fundamental shift in how family help teams engage with communities, recognising that informal, community-based support can be more responsive and effective than formal services. It therefore suggests that professional services need to enable, rather than crowd out, community support.
5. **Strengthening intervention powers**: 'Strengthen intervention powers and introduce Regional Improvement Commissioners to provide more robust challenge in the system' (p. 276). The review calls for structural reforms to children's social care and recommends appointing regional improvement commissioners to improve accountability within the system.

Whether in terms of amplifying children's voices, empowering practitioners and local authorities, or strengthening accountability within the system, the review report recognises the significance of power in shaping children's social care. In doing so, it inadvertently highlights the need to critically examine and work with power across the individual, professional and structural levels. To improve social care provision, therefore, practitioners, institutions and policy-makers must ensure that power is exercised in the best interests of those they serve. The following principles of PIP provide a foundation for this by offering a lens with which to understand and engage with power dynamics in social work contexts.

The five principles of PIP

Drawing on the PIP framework outlined in the previous chapter, the following five principles summarise its core insights to help professionals understand and engage with power in social work contexts.

1. Power is contextual and relational

Power is not a fixed entity, it is contextual and relational, meaning it changes depending on the circumstances and who is involved:

- power is contextual as it does not exist as a static force; rather, its expression and impact are contingent on situational factors where the access to and experience of power may shift depending on context;
- power is also relational because it exists within all social relationships and interactions; it is not something a person, institution or structural mechanism simply possesses – it is realised through interactions.

Practice implications: PIP requires practitioners to map power dynamics to understand who or what exercises power and in what context.

2. Power is exercised on three levels

The PIP approach identifies three levels at which power operates:

- *individual* (micro-level power): the power a person has over their own life and over others in their individual capacity, including their ability to make choices and carry out their will;
- *professional* (meso-level power): an additional layer of power which is exercised by professionals and institutions;
- *structural* (macro-level power): the social, political, legal, cultural and economic forces, as well as other mechanisms which channel power and can impact more broadly.

Practice implications: A power-informed approach requires an ongoing analysis of power at different levels: the individual/personal, the professional/institutional and the structural/societal levels.

3. Power is realised through action and inaction

Power is not only exercised through direct actions, but also through inaction, such as neglecting to provide support. When social workers choose not to intervene or remain silent about harmful policies/practices, they also exercise power:

- power is not solely realised through what is done, but also through what is not done at various levels – i.e., through omissions or failure to act;
- inaction can create impact in similar ways to action.

Practice implications: A critical understanding of inaction as a form of power is essential, as social workers need to recognise how inaction is not neutral; inaction can create impact in the same way that action can.

4. **Power creates positive, negative or dual impacts**

Power is not inherently good or bad in itself; its impact depends on how it is experienced by any given individual. The exercise of power can create a positive, negative, or dual impact:

- the impact of the exercise of power depends on how it is experienced by individuals;
- exercises of power do not always have a positive or negative effect; the effects can often be both positive and negative at the same time.

Practice implications: Critical assessment of the impact of power exercised through interventions is required as the positive, negative and dual impacts of power need to be identified to help social workers understand how their interactions may impact in productive, limiting or simultaneously limiting/productive ways.

5. **Past power influences present power**

The impact of power is not confined to any single moment in time; it operates across time and space, shaping how individuals experience power and agency throughout their lives. Social workers must therefore recognise how historical experiences of power intersect with present day experiences:

- an individual's past experiences of power (whether oppressive or enabling) shape their expectations, responses and ability to engage with power dynamics in the present;

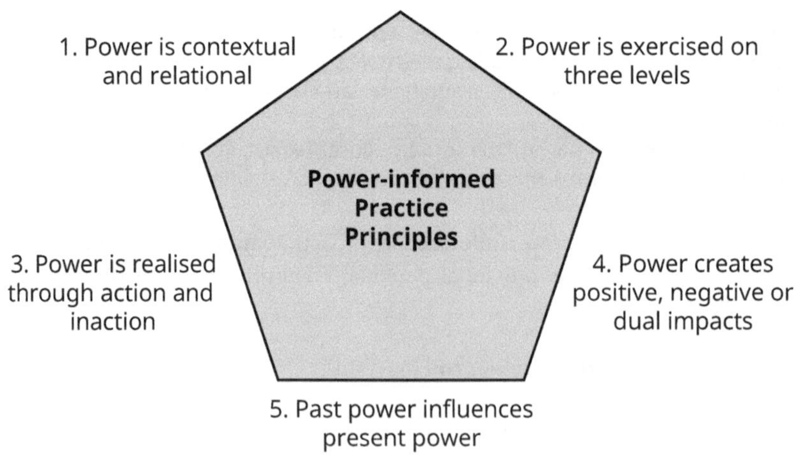

Figure 7.1 Power-informed practice principles

- service users who have experienced disempowerment (e.g., abuse, systemic exclusion, discrimination) may not trust those in positions of authority, affecting how they interact with professionals.

Practice implications: Social workers should consider how prior experiences of power may shape individual responses in the present.

For purposes of clarity, Figure 7.1 provides a visual representation of the five key principles of PIP.

Activity 7.1: Navigating the dual impact of power

The exercise of power often impacts in simultaneously limiting and productive ways and recognising this duality is essential for ethical and effective practice. When social workers recognise the duality of impact through the power they exercise, where power can be simultaneously limiting/productive, they should:

1. *be reflexive*: critically reflect on how decisions and actions (or inaction) impact service users while being aware of both the intended and unintended consequences of interventions;
2. *minimise harm, maximise benefit*: strive to reduce limiting effects and amplify productive impact while ensuring that interventions do not inadvertently disempower individuals;
3. *be transparent*: communicate openly with service users about the potential for limiting and productive impact as appropriate;
4. *co-create solutions*: where possible, co-create solutions with service users to address power imbalances and endeavour to ensure that decision-making reflects their agency, meets their needs and supports their aspirations.

By being reflexive, minimising harm, adopting transparency and co-creating solutions wherever possible, social workers can better navigate situations in which power has a dual impact. In doing so, they can reduce the negative effects of power, even when its impact is both limiting and productive at the same time.

The PIP model for social work

The following three-dimensional PIP model (See Figure 7.2) offers a standalone framework for embedding power-awareness into practice by integrating the five key principles into three key dimensions of social work engagement. The model places service users at the centre, while recognising the importance of establishing power-aware relationships, undertaking power-informed assessments and delivering empowering interventions.

The three-dimensional practice model is not intended to be applied in a fixed sequence; rather, it supports an iterative approach in which social workers continuously move between dimensions in response to evolving circumstances. Establishing power-aware relationships, for example, is not confined to the initial phase of engagement, but must be sustained and deepened throughout assessment and intervention. Similarly, power-informed assessments

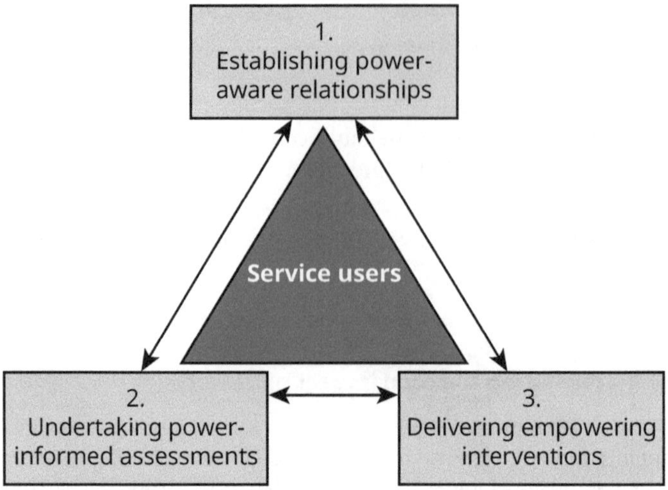

Figure 7.2 Power-informed practice model

are not one-off activities; they require ongoing adjustment based on new insights gained through interactions with service users. The dimension of delivering empowering interventions also feeds back into relationship-building and assessment, ensuring that practice remains responsive and dynamic. Ultimately, the three-dimensional practice model requires social workers to remain critically engaged with power throughout their practice.

Establishing power-aware relationships

Social workers must remain mindful of the inherent power imbalances between professionals and service users and should work to build and establish power-aware relationships. Central considerations within this dimension include recognising the contextual and relational nature of power (Principle 1) and understanding the multilevel exercise and impact of power (Principle 2) through action and inaction (Principle 3), as engaging with service users requires an awareness of how power exercised at the micro, meso and macro levels determines individual experiences (Principle 4). It is also essential for social workers to reflect on their own position of power, ensuring that their interactions remain sensitive to the ways in which past experiences of power continue to influence how service users experience power in the present (Principle 5). For example, service users who have experienced abuse often approach professional relationships with mistrust (Ferguson et al., 2020), therefore social workers must remain power-aware to ensure their practice acknowledges the enduring impact of past disempowerment and promotes autonomy and safety.

Undertaking power-informed assessments

Through power-informed assessments, practitioners can work towards developing an understanding of the service user's past and present experiences of power (Principle 5).

As part of the assessment process, social workers must recognise the positive, negative and dual impacts of power (Principle 4), which has been exercised through both action and inaction (Principle 3). Understanding how service users have experienced both oppressive and enabling forms of power in this way can help ensure that assessments do not inadvertently reinforce feelings of powerlessness. Wherever possible, therefore, social workers need to facilitate participatory assessments as service users should be involved in defining the issues they face and be involved in shaping the support they receive. This dimension of engagement can help to ensure that interventions are tailored not only to the immediate needs of service users, but also to the broader context of power relations (Principle 1 and 2).

Delivering empowering interventions

The third dimension of the practice model focuses on delivering empowering interventions. From a power-informed perspective, interventions should aim to restore agency to individuals by actively incorporating their wishes, feelings and perspectives into decision-making processes. At this stage, it is crucial to consider how past experiences of disempowerment continue to shape a service user's willingness and ability to engage with support (Principle 5). Wherever possible, therefore, interventions should be co-produced with strategies designed to rebuild autonomy, self-efficacy and confidence, as power is contextual and relational (Principle 1). Genuinely empowering interventions would also offer opportunities for long-term capacity-building alongside short-term, crisis-driven solutions. Additionally, social workers must recognise their own positional power and use this to advocate for wider change (Principle 2). This may include challenging exclusionary policies, addressing discriminatory practices and promoting power-conscious approaches within other professional settings. It is also essential that the power expressed through inaction is given equal consideration and that it is recognised as a form of decision-making that must be challenged if it is creating limiting impact (Principle 3). All interventions should also therefore be assessed in terms of their potential to be limiting, productive, or both, and service users should be informed of possible outcomes as appropriate (Principle 4).

As a collective, the PIP framework, its principles and the practice model can be used independently to guide power-informed social work. However, they can also be used in conjunction with existing social work approaches, complementing and enhancing established ways of understanding and responding to the needs of service users. The following section considers how social work approaches engage with power and how these can align with, or be strengthened by, a PIP perspective.

Social work approaches and PIP

Social work employs diverse approaches to understand and work through individual, community and systemic challenges in practice. However, without centring explicitly on power, social work approaches risk applying fragmented interventions which respond to presenting concerns rather than address root causes. After all, power is an intrinsic part of the human condition, shaping identities, relationships and life experiences. Whether explicitly acknowledged or not, power influences everything, including the distribution of resources, access to opportunities and the way individuals and communities experience oppression or privilege. Being 'power-informed', therefore, can help to ensure that all social work approaches contribute to meaningful, transformative practice as even well-intended interventions risk creating or reinforcing limiting impact when they do not explicitly address the issue of power.

Building on the recognition that power underlies all aspects of social work, it is important to examine how different social work approaches align with or may be enhanced by a power-informed perspective. This section begins to consider a number of key social work approaches through a power-informed lens. Some social work approaches explicitly challenge oppression and structural inequalities, while others focus more on individual empowerment. It is argued here that the power-informed perspective and its principles can be embedded within all social work approaches to ensure that power dynamics are critically examined and actively addressed across practice settings.

Ecological systems approach

The ecological approach to social work is rooted in Bronfenbrenner's ecological systems theory (1979), which sees human development as being shaped by interactions within multiple, interconnected systems, from immediate relationships to wider social structures. This theory was subsequently developed to create the *life model*, with a view to better understand how individuals and their social environment co-exist and interact (Germain and Gitterman, 1980). In social work practice, the approach emphasises the dynamic interaction between individuals and their environments, highlighting the power inherent in transactional processes (Ungar, 2002). Consequently, it enables practitioners to assess not only the person's needs, but also the environmental factors, including supports and barriers, that influence wellbeing across the micro, meso, exo, macro and chrono systems (Crawford, 2020). The ecological perspective in the UK underpins the assessment framework for children in need and their families, illustrated through the widely adopted *assessment triangle*. The triangle organises assessment around three interconnected domains: the child's developmental needs, parenting capacity and family and environmental factors (DoH, 2000, p. 17).

In similar ways to the PIP perspective, ecological social work approaches acknowledge that power operates within and between different systems (or levels). For example, parenting capacity may be constrained by issues such as poverty and discrimination, reflecting how macro-level systems exert power and shape individual experiences. Furthermore, both approaches consider the importance of relationships, contexts and power in social work practice. As a result, the ecological and PIP approaches are in favour of practice that addresses both the immediate needs of service users and wider concerns. Integrating a power-informed perspective into ecological approaches, therefore, can support social workers to recognise and challenge the multilevel power dynamics that shape the experiences of service users.

Highlights

- The ecological approach identifies how different systems interact to shape individual wellbeing in similar ways to the PIP perspective, where the different levels at which power operates and creates impact are recognised.
- Both approaches advocate for a holistic model of social work that moves beyond individualised interventions to also engage with broader concerns.
- The PIP perspective may enhance ecological approaches by facilitating a critical examination of how power operates within systems (expressed through both action and inaction) and how it can have limiting, productive, or dual impacts.

Strengths-based approaches

'A strengths-based approach explores, in a collaborative way the entire individual's abilities and their circumstances rather than making the deficit the focus of the intervention' (DoHSC, 2019, p. 24). Strengths-based approaches emphasise the capacities, resilience and resources of individuals and communities rather than focusing on perceived deficits. They encourage social workers to recognise the abilities, talents and aspirations of service users, even when these have been diminished by challenging circumstances, oppression, or trauma (Saleebey, 1996, 2013). In similar ways, the PIP perspective recognises that individuals can exercise power in productive ways.

Through its recognition of the operation of power at the individual, professional and structural levels, the PIP perspective can help to ensure that strengths-based approaches do not overlook the wider forces that influence an individual's capacity to exercise power. While strengths-based practice focuses on identifying and building upon existing abilities, the PIP approach can complement this by encouraging a critical examination of how power dynamics may support or constrain an individual's capacity to access resources, make choices and advocate for themselves. By promoting a critical awareness of structural inequalities, historical disempowerment and power imbalances, the PIP perspective can help to ensure that strengths-based approaches remain socially and contextually grounded rather than narrowly individualistic.

Highlights

- Strengths-based approaches and the PIP perspective both emphasise service user power and agency, recognising that everyone possesses power at the individual level, which can be used in productive ways.
- The PIP perspective can enhance strengths-based approaches by highlighting how power dynamics across the individual, professional and structural levels may prevent individuals from fully realising their strengths.

Empowerment approaches

Closely linked to strengths-based approaches, *empowerment* involves enabling individuals and communities to gain control over their circumstances and improve their wellbeing. Empowerment is recognised to be both a process and an outcome, which prioritises the redistribution of power from institutions to marginalised groups (Adams, 2017). Empowerment practices are grounded in a critical understanding of power across the personal, social and structural dimensions and emphasise the need to address the long-standing dehumanisation and marginalisation of communities (Ortega and Rodriguez-Jenkins, 2021). In similar ways, the power-informed perspective views empowerment as inherently connected to the relational, contextual and multilevel exercise of power and aligns with empowerment approaches through its recognition of how past experiences shape present dynamics.

From a PIP perspective, however, empowering individuals and communities requires a deeper exploration of how power is exercised or withheld across various levels and how these dynamics impact people in limiting, productive, or simultaneously limiting/productive ways. The paradoxical nature of empowerment, including its potential to contribute to disempowerment, has been noted (McLaughlin, 2016; Weidenstedt, 2016); adopting a PIP lens can help to ensure that empowerment practices do not inadvertently disempower individuals. With a clearer understanding of power, empowerment approaches may be strengthened in their capacity to challenge systemic inequalities, address historical injustices and redistribute power.

Highlights

- Empowerment approaches and the PIP perspective both highlight the importance of addressing power at multiple levels while also drawing connections between past experiences and present realities.
- A power-informed perspective may enhance empowerment approaches through its recognition of how power, channelled via efforts to empower individuals and communities, may have a limiting, productive, or simultaneously limiting/productive impact.
- The PIP lens can add to empowerment approaches through its recognition of how inaction is an expression of power and failure to act when required can contribute to experiences of disempowerment.

Anti-oppressive and anti-discriminatory practice

Anti-oppressive practice (AOP) and anti-discriminatory practice (ADP) approaches are closely related to the concept of empowerment as they seek to challenge oppression and discrimination and address the issue of power. AOP emphasises the intersectional nature of oppression, recognising that race, gender, class, disability and other social factors shape individuals' experiences within systems of power (Dalrymple and Burke, 2019). ADP also acknowledges the multifaceted nature of oppression and discrimination and how it is reproduced across the personal, cultural and structural levels within society (Thompson, 2016). However, such approaches have been critiqued for their impact on service users (Wilson and Beresford, 2000), while some argue that their mainstream adoption has weakened their 'critical edge', highlighting the need to explore alternative approaches for understanding and addressing power dynamics in social work practice (Cocker and Hafford-Letchfield, 2014).

The PIP perspective aligns with anti-oppressive approaches by recognising that power is contextual and relational, operates across multiple levels, and that past oppression (limiting expressions of power) shapes present experiences. PIP and AOP are also similar in that they both recognise the need to challenge oppressive power, but the PIP perspective takes this further by acknowledging that even well-intended social work interventions can often have both productive and limiting consequences. A PIP lens, therefore, encourages a more nuanced understanding of power, recognising that power has positive, negative and dual impacts and can be expressed through both action and inaction.

Highlights

- AOP/ADP approaches and the PIP perspective all emphasise the need to work on multiple levels to address oppression and discrimination (and power dynamics).
- A PIP perspective may strengthen AOP and ADP approaches by highlighting how efforts to address oppression and discrimination may impact in limiting, productive and simultaneously limiting/productive ways.
- AOP and ADP emphasise challenging oppression and discrimination; however, the PIP perspective highlights that failing to act is an expression of power and social workers must recognise that silence and neutrality can perpetuate oppression and discrimination.

Trauma-informed practice

Research on adverse childhood experiences (ACEs) has played a significant role in highlighting the long-term effects of childhood trauma, leading to an increased awareness within human services of its profound and lasting impact (Goddard, 2021). Subsequently, trauma-informed practice (TIP) has gained momentum in social work education (Cavener and Lonbay, 2022) and is widely adopted in social work practice as an approach to reduce the negative effects of trauma within the client–professional relationship (Levenson, 2017). As an approach, TIP promotes recognition of the signs and symptoms of trauma and its impact on an individual's wellbeing. It also emphasises the importance of creating culturally sensitive environments that foster safety, trust, choice, collaboration and empowerment (SAMHSA, 2014; OHID, 2022), with a view to prevent further trauma.

Being trauma-informed, means recognising that early life adversity is common among individuals and that many presenting issues are adaptive coping strategies shaped by past trauma. TIP highlights how trauma shapes core beliefs, affects psychosocial functioning and influences interactions with services (Levenson, 2017). The TIP approach also recognises that there is a need for practitioners to understand power imbalances and work to 'flatten the hierarchy' (RIP, 2018, p. 19). Levenson (2017, p. 5) highlights the importance of recognising such power dynamics in the helping relationship:

> *The inherent power imbalance in the helping relationship requires constant attention to the many (often subtle and insidious) ways that feelings of vulnerability and subsequent resistance can be generated for clients. Because many ACE survivors were betrayed by those who were supposed to protect and care for them, the helping relationship is fraught with potential for retraumatization when reminders of the capricious nature of past authority figures are activated.*

TIP and PIP share key features, as both acknowledge the influence of power dynamics and the impact of past experiences on current realities and interactions. However, while TIP focuses on the psychological and emotional symptoms of trauma, the PIP perspective views trauma (except that which arises from natural causes) as resulting from limiting expressions of power. Understanding trauma through a power-informed lens can therefore enable a more nuanced approach to support by recognising power as central to both trauma and recovery. Additionally, being power-informed can strengthen TIP through its recognition of how power can have positive, negative, or dual impacts through action and inaction. Recognising this can help to ensure that interventions are mindfully developed to prevent retraumatisation or, at the very least, make explicit any limiting impact. It has also been noted that, when applied in isolation, TIP risks pathologising individuals by focusing solely on trauma responses, without addressing the broader conditions that perpetuate harm (Smith and Monteux, 2023). The PIP perspective can therefore enhance TIP as it encourages professionals to engage with power relations and the root causes of trauma at all levels.

Highlight

- TIP and PIP both recognise the role of power and how past experiences influence interactions in the present.
- While TIP focuses on the emotional and psychological effects of trauma, the PIP perspective highlights how harmful uses of power can result in trauma – and emphasises that addressing power is integral to the healing process.
- Where TIP focuses on the individual relationship, PIP encourages practitioners to actively engage with power relations at all levels.

Person-centred approaches

Rooted in humanistic psychology (Rogers, 1951), a person-centred approach encourages social workers to focus on the individual needs, goals and aspirations of service users, to ensure they remain central to all interventions (Lindsey et al., 2013). This approach requires practitioners to foster trusting relationships, validate personal experiences and promote self-determination, with a view to enabling individuals to actively participate in decisions affecting their lives. However, while person-centred approaches emphasise individual agency, they often overlook the broader social, systemic and structural forces that shape a person's ability to exercise autonomy (van Breda, 2022). A PIP lens can therefore enhance person-centred practice as it draws attention to how individual empowerment is shaped by the broader contexts in which power operates.

Whereas person-centred approaches promote autonomy and self-determination, the PIP perspective requires practitioners to critically examine how power relations either enable or restrict a person's ability to make meaningful choices. This is particularly relevant in social work, where the value of non-directive support is emphasised, yet professionals are often required to make decisions that direct the course of interventions (Murphy et al., 2013). Without careful consideration of the potential impacts of expressions of power (whether positive, negative, or dual), professional decisions may unintentionally undermine autonomy rather than enhance it. A power-informed approach can therefore strengthen person-centred practice by ensuring that practitioners do not focus solely on individual agency, but also engage with the broader factors that shape a person's choices.

Highlights

- Both the person-centred approach and the PIP perspective recognise self-determination as expressions of individual power.
- A PIP lens may enhance person-centred thinking through its recognition of how individual agency is deeply linked to broader power dynamics which may restrict autonomy and choice.
- While person-centred practice is inherently non-directive, the PIP perspective can help social workers to recognise how power shapes decision-making and influences interventions to ensure that person-centred approaches align with the practice realities of social work.

Relationship-based practice

Relationship-based practice (RBP) is defined by three key characteristics. First, it sees the relationship between the social worker and service user as the primary vehicle for change, emphasising human connection over interventions. Second, this relationship is recognised to be dynamic, sometimes therapeutic, yet inherently imbalanced, as the social worker holds authority while offering support. Third, relational social work acknowledges that both practitioners and service users are influenced by personal and structural contexts, with experiences, emotions and societal factors shaping interactions (Winter, 2019). Here, RBP acknowledges the influence of contextual factors such as power dynamics, professional roles, poverty, social exclusion and political ideology (Ingram and Smith, 2018), highlighting the need for social workers to understand and navigate these influences to achieve positive outcomes.

RBP and the PIP perspective both recognise that effective social work extends beyond standardised interventions, emphasising the relational nature of practice and the influence of broader contextual dynamics (including power relations) on service users' experiences and interactions. Based on trust and cooperation, relational approaches view the relationship between the social worker and service user as the primary vehicle for change; however, from a power-informed perspective, trust is not something that automatically develops through connection. Service users who have experienced disempowerment or limiting expressions of power in the past may struggle to build trusting relationships in the present. Therefore, applying a PIP lens can support RBP by prompting social workers to identify and address power imbalances that may limit trust and engagement.

RBP recognises that social workers hold authority, but the PIP perspective takes this further by emphasising the ethical responsibility to use power reflexively, given that power can have positive, negative, or dual impact and may be exercised through both action and inaction. RBP has been critiqued for its overemphasis on maintaining positive relationships, which may lead to challenges in fulfilling professional responsibilities (Murphy et al., 2013). A power-informed lens, therefore, may help ensure that social workers also consider how failing to act or avoiding difficult conversations due to the desire to preserve relationships with service users may result in harm, because inaction can also create negative or dual impacts.

Highlights

- Both RBP and the PIP approach emphasise the importance of relationships and recognise how effective social work goes beyond standard interventions.
- The PIP perspective can strengthen relational social work by encouraging a critical examination of power dynamics, recognising that relationships are influenced by prior experiences of power.
- A power-informed lens may enhance RBP with its recognition of how inaction, or avoiding difficult conversations to preserve relationships can cause a negative or dual impact.

Activity 7.2: The limits and constraints of social work power

a. **Levels of power and social work practice**

While social workers hold professional status, their power and influence can often be limited. Structural barriers, institutional policies and funding constraints are among the key factors that shape the contexts in which social workers operate. A power-informed approach recognises that power is contextual and relational; acknowledging that although social workers can effect change they are also frequently constrained by external forces beyond their control.

The PIP approach recognises that power is exercised on multiple levels: micro (individual), meso (professional) and macro (structural). Social workers often find themselves navigating tensions between these levels, where external factors may limit the scope of their influence and ability to effect change. For instance, advocating for a service user's needs may be hindered by restrictive organisational policies or funding shortages. Recognising these limitations should not lead to inaction, but rather highlight the importance of adopting a reflexive and realistic approach – one that acknowledges both the capacity and the constraints of professional influence.

A power-informed approach encourages social workers to be critically aware of these dilemmas, recognising that, while they cannot do everything, they can still work strategically to minimise harm and maximise benefit within their scope of influence. By adopting a power-informed lens, social workers can exercise even the most limited power with purpose and integrity to contribute to positive change.

b. **Intersectionality and professional power**

The power held by social workers is shaped by both professional authority and intersecting social identities. While social workers have access to a degree of professional power, they are not exempt from broader societal power structures such as gender, race or class etc. Intersectionality – the recognition that individuals experience overlapping and interconnected forms of oppression and privilege – provides a critical lens for understanding how professional power interacts with these broader systems (Crenshaw, 1989).

For example, a female social worker may have access to professional power in her role, yet she can still experience patriarchal power dynamics when working with male colleagues or service users. Despite her professional position, societal norms around gender may influence how she is perceived and treated, potentially undermining her authority or requiring her to navigate additional barriers to establish credibility. Similarly, a social worker from a minoritised ethnic background may experience racialised power dynamics when engaging with colleagues or service users, which can affect their sense of power and professional influence.

Reflective questions

1. How can external forces shape the ways in which social workers are either able or unable to advocate for service users and influence outcomes?
2. When professional power is limited by external constraints, in what ways can social workers minimise harm and effect positive change within the scope of their influence?
3. How can intersecting social identities influence how social workers experience and exercise professional power?

Activity 7.3: Power-informed supervision in social work

Supervision within social work is intended to be a process of receiving support and guidance from a supervisor, manager, mentor, or colleague. This includes discussing current cases and related challenges, reflecting on practice to facilitate learning and reviewing decisions to ensure they comply with legal and statutory requirements (SWE, 2025). In reality, however, traditional case management approaches to supervision may reinforce hierarchical power structures, where authority flows one way, from supervisor to supervisee. A power-informed approach reimagines supervision as a relational and reflexive process, which acknowledges and explores power dynamics at multiple levels.

Adopting a power-informed approach to supervision would recognise that both supervisors and supervisees bring their own experiences, positionality and constraints to the supervisory relationship. Rather than simply directing or evaluating, supervisors could foster an open, collaborative environment where power is acknowledged rather than assumed. It would also involve engaging in reflective discussions about how power shapes decision-making, organisational culture and interactions with service users. By acknowledging and critically engaging with power, supervisors can foster a space that is not only supportive, but also empowering for social work practitioners.

Reflective questions

1. In what ways do power dynamics (both visible and hidden) shape your experience of supervision, either as a supervisee or supervisor?
2. How does your own positionality, identity and organisational context influence how you engage with supervision and make decisions in practice?
3. What are the possible advantages of speaking openly about power within supervision?

Summary

This chapter has provided an in-depth exploration of power-informed practice (PIP) as a critical approach for social work. It began by highlighting the importance of power within social care, before introducing the five principles of PIP, offering a foundation for understanding power within social work contexts. Following this, the discussion extended to how the PIP framework and its principles can be translated into a standalone approach which requires practitioners to establish power-aware relationships, undertake power-informed assessments and deliver empowering interventions. The chapter also explored how the PIP perspective can potentially enhance existing social work approaches.

The chapter went on to highlight the limits of professional power, recognising that social workers operate within wider structures and systems that can often restrict their influence. The role of intersectionality was briefly examined, emphasising how professional power intersects with other social identities, such as gender and ethnicity. And, finally, the chapter introduced the idea of power-informed supervision as a means of supporting social workers within their practice. It is suggested that by adopting a power-informed lens social workers can more effectively navigate their roles, challenge oppression, foster empowerment and contribute to meaningful change for individuals, communities and society at large.

8 Working with child victims of abuse: A power-informed approach

Introduction

Whatever its form, child abuse can impact on children in extremely detrimental ways (see Chapters 3 and 4). Depending on their role, social workers have a range of professional responsibilities, explicitly outlined in the law, or as part of broader obligations, to intervene when children are at risk of, or have been subjected to harm (see Chapter 2). Building on previous discussions, this chapter explores how social workers can engage with children who have experienced abuse in power-informed ways. The chapter begins by examining the progressive role of professional power in responding to child abuse in England, from prevention efforts to legal intervention. Additionally, the chapter outlines key ethical considerations when undertaking direct work with children, including confidentiality, informed consent and acting in the child's best interests. This is followed by guidance for social workers who work directly with children who have experienced abuse, based on the three-dimensional power-informed practice (PIP) model introduced in the previous chapter. This includes a child-centred focus on establishing power-aware relationships, undertaking power-informed assessments and delivering empowering interventions. In doing so, the chapter aims to support social workers in using their professional power to work with and empower children who have experienced abuse.

Professional power and child abuse

In legal and policy contexts, the terms 'child' and 'young person' are defined differently depending on age and purpose. Under the Children Act 1989, a child is legally defined as anyone under the age of 18 (Section 105); however, the term 'young person' is more flexible and context-dependent. For example, the National Youth Agency defines young people as those aged between 11 and 19, but this can extend up to the age of 25 depending on individual needs and circumstances (NYA, 2024). These definitional variations recognise adolescence as a transitional phase during which individuals may no longer legally be classified as children, but still require developmentally appropriate support into adulthood. Understanding these nuances is essential, as age and developmental stage significantly influence the nature of professional intervention, the legal thresholds that apply and the degree of power a child or young person may be able to exercise. For the purposes of consistency and clarity, the chapter focuses on the support which may be provided to children under 18, while acknowledging that, in practice, support may extend beyond this age.

Child protection initiatives in the UK follow a continuum in which professional authority and involvement increase in response to the level of concern. They begin with preventative measures aimed at supporting families and safeguarding children from harm. As concerns grow, these efforts may advance to statutory involvement, including legal proceedings. In the most serious cases, this can result in the removal of a child from their family environment, if such action is deemed necessary to promote the child's safety and wellbeing. The following offers an overview of the stages of prevention and intervention in England, reflecting the incremental increase in power that is exercised on a professional level, when addressing child abuse within the UK context.

Prevention efforts (minimal power)

Prevention efforts reflect the lowest level of professional authority in the context of child protection – that is, minimal power. The purpose of prevention efforts is to reduce risk factors and strengthen families before significant problems emerge (NSPCC, 2023). This highlights the role of universal services (such as education and healthcare) and other organisations in providing support and guidance, reinforcing the importance of safeguarding as a broader concept within which child protection is one component (DfE, 2023) rather than its entirety. Prevention strategies may include the likes of public campaigns on child safeguarding and protection or community-based family support initiatives. At this level, families engage with services of their own accord, meaning that there is no compulsion and minimal professional power is exercised.

Early help (subtle power)

'Early Help is the total support that improves a family's resilience and outcomes or reduces the chance of a problem getting worse' (DLUHC, 2022, p. 7). Early help assessments (EHAs) may be undertaken to identify needs and enable families to connect with the right support at the earliest opportunity. As part of the process, multiagency support plans may be developed, with professionals encouraging families to access services which may be required. At this level, families can choose to accept or decline support. Although professionals may subtly leverage their professional power to guide decisions, they cannot enforce engagement.

Child in need (Section 17 – moderate power)

Under Section 17 of the Children Act 1989, local authorities have a statutory duty to safeguard and promote the welfare of children in need. This includes providing a range of targeted services to support children whose health or development is likely to be significantly impaired without intervention. The process typically involves conducting child in need assessments and developing multiagency support plans, led by social workers but involving other professional services. This statutory intervention allows services to support children and families without the child's removal from their home environment being a present concern. At this stage, professional power and influence are moderate, typically increasing only when families do not engage or when support fails to reduce the risk of harm to the child.

Child protection (Section 47 – enhanced power)

Formal child protection interventions begin under Section 47 of the Children Act 1989, which places a duty on local authorities to investigate when there is reasonable cause to suspect that a child is suffering, or is likely to suffer, significant harm due to abuse or neglect. At this stage, social workers convene strategy discussions involving the police, health professionals, education providers and other relevant agencies to share information and decide on actions. The outcome of these discussions determines whether a Section 47 enquiry is initiated to assess the level of risk to the child (DfE, 2023, p. 86). If the enquiry substantiates concerns, an initial child protection conference (ICPC) is held, leading to the development of a child protection plan. These plans require active engagement from parents or carers and are monitored through statutory visits and multiagency review meetings. Because the child is now recognised as suffering or at risk of suffering significant harm, professionals are granted enhanced power. Parental cooperation is expected, and persistent non-compliance or lack of engagement can lead to legal proceedings.

Immediate protection (emergency power)

In situations where a child is at risk of immediate harm and requires urgent protection, emergency powers are available to the local authority and police to remove the child from danger. Police protection powers under Section 46 of the Children Act 1989 allow the police to remove a child for up to 72 hours in emergency situations. An emergency protection order (EPO) from the courts grants local authorities temporary parental responsibility (PR) for up to eight days to ensure that the child is protected (Section 44, Children Act 1989). At this level, professional power overrides the individual power of parents and caregivers due to the structural power channelled through the court system on the basis of legislation.

Court orders (maximum power)

Where children are deemed to be at ongoing risk of significant harm and require long-term protection, the local authority may use its professional/institutional power to initiate court proceedings to ensure the child is either intensively supervised or removed (temporarily or permanently) from their home environment through legal orders. Practice Direction 12A, commonly referred to as the Public Law Outline (PLO), sets out the responsibilities of local authorities when considering an application to the court for an order (Ministry of Justice, 2023). At this stage, several legal options are available to the local authority to maximise their power under the Children Act 1989:

- *supervision orders* (Section 35) do not grant the local authority parental responsibility; however, they provide a legal framework enabling the authority to monitor the child's welfare, 'advise, assist and befriend' the child and support compliance with any conditions imposed by the court;
- *interim care orders* (Section 38) provide the local authority with shared parental responsibility on a temporary basis. This allows them to make decisions about the child's welfare and, where necessary, override parental decisions to protect the child. An interim care order can last up to eight weeks initially and may be renewed for periods of up to 28 days thereafter;
- *care orders* (Section 33) provide the local authority with shared parental responsibility on a long-term basis. Parents retain parental responsibility, but the local authority has overriding decision-making power over the child's upbringing, including where the child lives, their education and medical treatment. The local authority may therefore restrict the parents' involvement in such decisions, if necessary, to safeguard or promote the child's welfare. A care order lasts until the child turns 18, unless it is discharged earlier by the court.

Long-term planning (reconfiguring power)

Children subject to care orders may be considered to be in *long-term care* when the plan is for them to remain *looked after* for the foreseeable future. In such circumstances, the local authority's aim is to promote the child's stability and wellbeing and secure the best long-term outcomes for them. At this stage, local authorities have the opportunity to re-evaluate how decision-making power is distributed in relation to the child's care and welfare. If risks reduce in the family environment and it is deemed to be in the child's best interests, the local authority may consider reunification at any point – that is, returning the child to their parents and transferring power back to them. However, if reunification is not appropriate there are a range of options available to the local authority to enable them to reconfigure decision-making power in order to support children's wellbeing and long-term stability:

- *long-term fostering or residential care*: children remain looked after by the local authority, which retains parental responsibility and holds ultimate decision-making power. Although carers provide daily care and support, they do not have legal parental responsibility and therefore cannot make major decisions unless authority is formally delegated. In practice, some decision-making power is delegated to carers, particularly for day-to-day matters, but legal authority remains with the local authority (DfE, 2014);

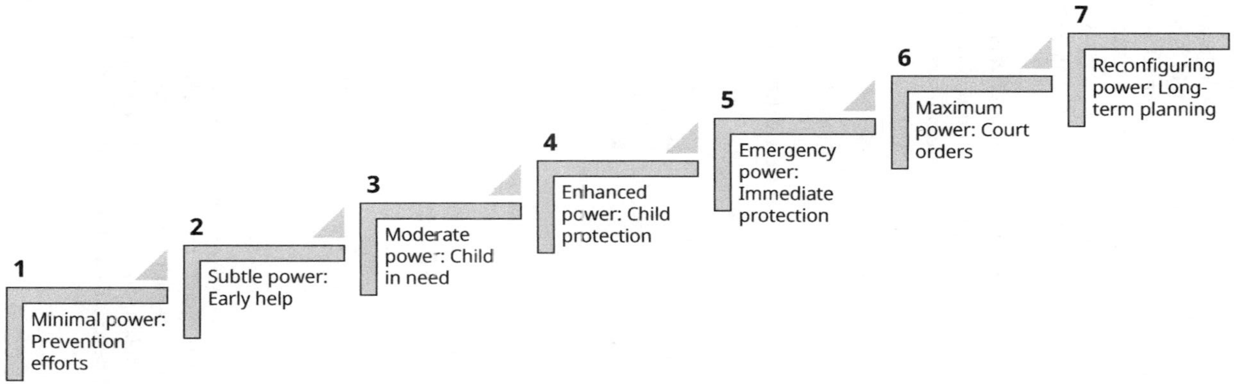

Figure 8.1 Progressive escalation of professional power

- *special guardianship order* (SGO): under Section 14A of the Children Act 1989, an SGO grants enhanced parental responsibility to a relative, close family friend, or foster carer until the child turns 18. While birth parents retain limited parental responsibility, the special guardian holds primary decision-making power. Once an SGO is granted, the local authority typically withdraws from active oversight unless concerns arise. However, while SGOs can arise from care proceedings, they do not require a care order to be initiated or granted;
- *adoption*: permanently transfers full parental responsibility to the adoptive parents, either with the birth parents' consent or through a *placement order* under Sections 21–4 of the Adoption and Children Act 2002. Once an *adoption order* has been granted by the court, the birth parents and the local authority lose all legal parental rights. Power is therefore fully transferred to the adoptive family, through the creation of a new legal parent–child relationship.

Essentially, the child protection framework in England reflects a commitment to the principle that state intervention in family life should be limited to the minimum necessary to safeguard children from harm (DfE, 2021b). Figure 8.1 (see page 95) illustrates the progressive escalation of professional power in response to child abuse-related concerns.

Activity 8.1: The no order principle – to do nothing is to do something

The Children Act 1989, the Children (Scotland) Act 1995 and the Children (Northern Ireland) Order 1995 state that courts should not issue an order unless doing so would be better for the child than making no order at all, even when they have the authority to do so. The *no order principle* is enshrined in Section 1(5) of the Children Act 1989, which stipulates:

> *Where a court is considering whether or not to make one or more orders under this Act with respect to a child, it shall not make the order or any of the orders unless it considers that doing so would be better for the child than making no order at all.*

The no order principle serves three key purposes:

- *limiting unnecessary legal intervention*: it discourages the use of court orders unless they are essential to addressing a specific issue. While legal intervention can protect children, unnecessary court involvement may impact negatively on children and families;
- *ensuring the child's welfare takes priority*: orders should only be granted if they are likely to improve a child's wellbeing, rather than simply because legal grounds exist. For instance, in care proceedings a court may determine that placing a child in local authority care through a care order is not in their best interests;
- *reducing unnecessary applications*: it aims to prevent cases from being brought to court without a clear need, ensuring legal interventions are only pursued when absolutely required.

(Open University, n.d.)

The no order principle recognises that choosing not to intervene is an expression of power in itself. In applying this principle, courts demonstrate that inaction can be as impactful as action, shaping outcomes by limiting unnecessary state control. The no order principle thus serves as a mechanism for balancing power, ensuring that legal authority is exercised proportionately and ethically, with the child's welfare remaining the central concern.

Reflective questions

1. What does the no order principle teach us about the power of inaction in social work; how do you recognise when choosing not to act in a particular way may be in the child's best interest?
2. How can social workers ensure that any recommendation for legal intervention is genuinely necessary and proportionate?

Ethical considerations when working with children

When supporting children who have experienced abuse, social workers must be mindful of their ethical responsibilities to ensure the child's safety and promote their wellbeing in accordance with professional codes of practice (BASW, 2021; SWE, 2019). This requires balancing legal, professional and moral responsibilities, particularly in relation to confidentiality, informed consent and acting in the child's best interests. It is recognised that there is often insufficient focus on the power imbalances between vulnerable groups and the bureaucratic systems mandated to intervene when a child's safety is at risk (Lonne et al., 2016). Social workers therefore play a vital role in upholding ethical principles, even in the face of complex and challenging circumstances.

Confidentiality and information sharing

Confidentiality is a core ethical principle in social work which fosters a sense of safety and support for individuals when they are sharing personal information (Millstein, 2000). However, in cases of child abuse, confidentiality must be balanced against safeguarding responsibilities. Social workers must therefore ensure that children are informed about the limits of confidentiality, while sharing information with others on a need-to-know basis. Statutory guidance (DfE, 2023) emphasises that notions of confidentiality should never pose a barrier to preventing harm, particularly when a child is at risk. In applying the UK General Data Protection Regulation (GDPR) and the Data Protection Act (DPA, 2018), social workers are permitted to share information for safeguarding purposes without consent, provided there is a lawful basis for doing so, such as fulfilling a legal obligation or performing a public task (ICO, n.d.). However, information sharing must be proportionate and children's rights should be respected as far as possible in such circumstances.

Informed consent

Obtaining informed consent in an age-appropriate manner is a fundamental ethical consideration when working with children. Social workers must be mindful of a child's evolving capacity to understand and make decisions, particularly in situations where parental involvement may not be in the child's best interests. The Gillick competence framework (Gillick v West Norfolk and Wisbech AHA [1985] UKHL 7) provides guidance on assessing whether a child has the maturity and understanding to consent to specific interventions. Legally, a 'child' is defined as an individual aged 0–18, but Gillick competence primarily applies to those under 16. Once a child turns 16, they are generally considered capable of making decisions on various matters, as outlined in different statutes (Phillimore, 2020). However, even if a child lacks the capacity to consent, they still have the right to be informed and to express their views on decisions that affect them. Social workers should therefore seek the child's consent wherever possible, while also obtaining consent from parents or guardians when appropriate.

Best interests of children

The Children Act 1989 emphasises that the welfare of the child must be the paramount consideration in all decisions regarding their care and protection. The principle of *best interests* requires social workers to prioritise children's wellbeing, ensuring that interventions are both necessary and proportionate. When working with children who have experienced abuse, social workers must consider the child's emotional and developmental needs and ensure that their actions promote wellbeing and do not cause further harm.

Research suggests that understandings of children's best interests are heavily influenced by assumptions about their emotional needs, which are often connected to family relationships and are predominantly interpreted through the lens of attachment theory. As a result, professional decisions often prioritise stability over change, with children's distress during separation, indiscriminate affection and challenging behaviours often being viewed as evidence of attachment problems that require stable caregiving arrangements (Keddell, 2016). In some cases, this focus on stability may cloud professional judgement, as social workers may well overlook the potential negative impact of leaving children with their families. While stability is important for children, social workers must navigate the dual impact of power, where the act of removal may be necessary for safety, but also disrupts the child's family life. This highlights the importance of social workers remaining critically aware of how their decisions influence a child's wellbeing, when professional power is exercised and can impact in simultaneously limiting/productive ways.

Children's wishes and feelings

Section 53 of the Children Act 2004 requires local authorities to ascertain and consider the 'wishes and feelings' of children as far as is reasonably practicable when carrying out their duties. However, due to the absence of clear statutory guidance on participation, many children miss opportunities to be involved in their own protection planning (Dillon, 2021). Social workers must therefore actively listen to children and consider their wishes and feelings when making decisions about their care and protection. It is essential that social workers recognise the inherent power imbalance between professionals and children and strive to ensure that the child's voice is central to the decision-making process because:

> *Children do not need to be given a voice, as they already have one. Furthermore, they are able to articulate their voice, but power asymmetries between children and adults oftentimes limit them in doing so. Thus, making their voice 'invisible'.*
>
> (Nunes, 2021, p. 433)

The tension between promoting children's participation and operating within child protection systems that are not structurally designed for their direct involvement has long been recognised (Sanders and Mace, 2006) and continues to present a significant challenge. Despite these constraints, however, social workers have an ethical and professional responsibility to ensure that children's views and preferences inform assessments, planning and decision-making as far as possible.

Transparency

Social workers have an ethical responsibility to be as transparent as possible during their interventions, which includes clearly explaining the purpose of their involvement and any consequences within child and family social work practice (Dons et al., 2022). This means not only clarifying the reasons for their engagement, but also explaining what children and families can expect from the intervention. In doing so, social workers must provide information that is both accessible and developmentally appropriate, enabling children to understand their rights and the steps being taken on their behalf. However, while social workers recognise the importance of explaining the reasoning, timing and processes behind their decisions, they also acknowledge the practical difficulties in fully implementing transparency on a practice level (Devlieghere and Gillingham, 2021). Nevertheless, transparency remains an important ethical obligation and social workers are required to be as transparent as possible when engaging with children and families.

In addition to ethical considerations such as confidentiality, informed consent, acting in the child's best interests, incorporating children's views and being transparent, social workers must also be responsive to the cultural contexts in which children and adults are situated. Cultural perspectives can influence how child abuse is understood, experienced and addressed (NSPCC, 2014), and the following discussion examines the evolution of cultural perspectives in social work and their ongoing significance.

Activity 8.2: Cultural perspectives in social work

Recognising the diversity within communities and actively addressing the effects of inequality and discrimination is a key standard for social work practice (Standard 1.5, SWE, 2019). Within social work, navigating cultural differences requires more than simply good intentions – it necessitates an integration of cultural awareness, knowledge and skills over time (Laird and Tedam, 2019). Social work perspectives relating to working within different cultural contexts have gradually evolved over time from notions of *cultural sensitivity*, to *cultural competence* and more recently to the concept of *cultural humility*.

(Continued)

The concept of cultural sensitivity emphasises the need for cultural awareness and respect towards diverse cultural practices and values, which includes avoiding assumptions, stereotypes and personal bias (Cowden and Singh, 2013). However, cultural sensitivity alone risks remaining superficial if it does not translate to practice-based applications. The idea of cultural competence, therefore, builds on this concept, by highlighting the need for culturally sound practices to be established on the individual, institutional and societal levels (NASW, 2025).

Cultural competence in social work involves reflecting on one's own cultural perspective and identity, while actively acquiring the knowledge, values and skills to effectively work with individuals in practice. Laird and Tedam (2019, p. 94), offer the following process model for cultural competence:

- *cultural awareness*: recognising how personal values and beliefs influence how we perceive people from different cultural backgrounds;
- *cultural skill*: the ability to gather, understand and accurately interpret cultural information within assessments and care planning;
- *cultural knowledge*: seeking out information and learning about other cultures, faiths and ethnic backgrounds in a way which avoids stereotyping;
- *cultural encounter*: moving past surface-level interactions with families from diverse ethnic backgrounds to engage in meaningful, cross-cultural experiences that alter the practitioner's existing beliefs regarding particular groups;
- *cultural desire*: a practitioner's authentic, self-driven motivation to engage with the previous four processes willingly, rather than as a result of external pressure or obligation.

The concept of cultural competence has, however, generated considerable debate, primarily because it rests on the problematic assumption that social workers can acquire complete knowledge of every aspect of a given 'culture' (Williams and Lee, 2024), raising questions about whether true cultural competence can ever be achieved. More recently, therefore, the concept of cultural humility has been introduced to highlight the importance of self-reflection and lifelong learning. It is suggested that, 'cultural humility is fundamentally distinct from that of competence, representing a state of being open and teachable, versus that of being effective' (Gottlieb, 2020, p. 471) and can be broken down into three key principles:

1. committing to an ongoing process of self-awareness and enquiry, supported by a diverse community of trusted colleagues;
2. remaining open to learning and working to understand cultures from the perspective of clients rather than relying solely on preconceptions;
3. continuously reflecting on the social systems and their inherent distributions of power and privilege that shape both the realities of social workers and clients.

(Gottlieb, 2020)

To summarise, while notions of cultural sensitivity laid the groundwork by promoting cultural awareness and respect, the idea of cultural competence pushed practitioners to actively develop the necessary knowledge and skills for enhanced service delivery. However, the limitations inherent in trying to master every facet of a culture have led to the development of cultural humility as a concept, which shifts from notions of mastery to accountability, 'which takes into account the fluidity of culture and challenges both individuals and institutions to address inequalities' (Fisher-Borne et al., 2014, p. 165).

Reflective questions

1. What are the key differences between cultural sensitivity, competence and humility?
2. In what ways might cultural understandings enhance child protection practices in social work?

Power-informed practice: guidance for social workers supporting children who have experienced abuse

The following guidance is based on the principles of PIP and the three-dimensional practice model outlined in Chapter 7. It is intended to support professionals undertaking direct work with child victims of abuse, particularly those who are verbally communicative and have been assessed as capable of understanding the context of professional involvement. When working with younger children, or children with additional needs, a power-informed perspective may be incorporated into the overall approach which is adopted to ensure that children are supported in a way that aligns with their specific needs.

Social workers may engage with child victims of abuse in various settings, including schools, health services, voluntary organisations and local authority children's social care. Given the diversity in social work roles and responsibilities, the following guidance is intentionally designed to be broad and promote flexibility, which allows social workers to engage with children in power-informed ways, irrespective of the nature of their involvement. The guidance, therefore, is by no means intended to be prescriptive, fixed or exhaustive; instead, it offers a foundation for developing power-informed practice, which must remain flexible, responsive and tailored to the unique experiences and needs of every child.

It is also important to recognise that children do not exist in isolation; they are embedded within family systems that may include parents or caregivers, siblings and extended family, all of whom can significantly influence their experiences. From a power-informed perspective, social workers must remain critically aware of how power operates within these relationships, recognising that family members can exercise individual power in ways that either support or undermine a child's wellbeing. While this broader context is acknowledged, the following guidance specifically focuses on direct work with children, structured around the three dimensions of the practice model outlined in the previous chapter: establishing power-aware relationships, undertaking power-informed assessments and delivering empowering interventions. The broader familial context is then considered in the subsequent case study.

Establishing power-aware relationships with children

It is suggested that establishing power-aware relationships is crucial when supporting children who have experienced abuse. Such relationships can provide a foundation for rebuilding trust by acknowledging both empowering and disempowering experiences that may influence a child's capacity to connect with others. Research suggests that developing trust can be achieved when service users feel listened to, and practitioners adjust their approach in ways that respect their needs (Ferguson et al., 2020). The following strategies are suggested for building power-aware relationships with children by acknowledging past experiences of power, adopting transparency and fostering trust through consistency and reliability.

Acknowledge the child's past experiences of power and powerlessness

Social workers must recognise that abuse is an exercise of limiting power, which often leaves children feeling disempowered, silenced and distrustful of others. A child's previous experience of those misusing power will influence how they respond to professionals because past experiences of power impact on the present. Social workers therefore need to:

- acknowledge children's past experiences of power to demonstrate empathy and understanding;
- validate children's feelings and experiences by actively listening and making appropriate adjustments whenever possible;
- recognise that if children appear to be withdrawn or resistant these responses stem from their past experiences of limiting/negative expressions of power.

Adopt transparency as appropriate

The concept of *transparency*, which advocates for openness, trust and collaborative relationships with service users, is commonly referred to in social work (Devlieghere and Gillingham, 2021). However, due to ethical and legal obligations, complete transparency may not always be appropriate when working with children. To achieve an appropriate level of transparency, social workers can:

- explain who they are and what their role is using clear, child-friendly language;
- explain confidentiality and its limits in an age-appropriate way;
- be upfront about their decision-making power and its limits.

Foster trust through consistency and reliability

Building trust with children who have experienced abuse requires social workers to demonstrate consistency and reliability throughout their engagement. This means following through on commitments, communicating clearly and honestly and creating a stable environment that helps children feel safe. Social workers therefore need to:

- follow through on commitments to build trust;
- provide clear, honest updates about what is happening and what will happen next, helping to reduce uncertainty;
- remain available, consistent and dependable throughout their involvement.

Undertaking power-informed assessments

It is suggested that effective assessments must go beyond identifying a child's immediate needs to reflect a deeper understanding of how power operates at various levels and influences their life. Therefore, it is proposed that social workers consider the individual, professional and structural dimensions that shape a child's experiences. The following guidance outlines practical approaches for exploring these layers of power and impact within the assessment process.

Recognise how power operates at multiple levels

For the purposes of assessment, it is important for social workers to recognise the different levels at which power is exercised to influence children's experiences. As part of the assessment process, social workers should consider the following:

- *individual/personal power*: identifying how power is experienced by the child within their immediate relationships, including those with parents, carers, siblings, peers and others;
- *professional/institutional power*: recognising how education, health and other professional organisations exercise power over the child's life, while remaining mindful of how social work involvement is also being experienced by the child;
- *structural/societal power*: recognising how power at the structural/societal level shapes the child's experiences and sense of agency – for example, through legal frameworks, cultural norms and broader social forces.

Explore how power has been used in limiting ways

As part of the assessment process, exploring how power has been used in limiting ways against a child can help identify what made them feel powerless and how. In practice, this means that social workers must be skilled in assessing the power dynamics that affect children and understand how these dynamics may contribute to feelings of powerlessness. Social workers can begin to map and assess children's experiences of limiting power by:

- engaging with children through age-appropriate activities, such as storytelling, drawing, or play, to help them express difficult experiences, thoughts and feelings;
- exploring situations where children may have felt powerless and why – for example, at home, in school, or other environments;
- considering children's experiences of limiting power related to broader factors such as ethnicity, socioeconomic status, gender and disability within assessments.

Explore how power has been used in productive ways

As part of the assessment, it is equally important to capture the positive expressions and experiences of power in a child's life. Social workers can therefore:

- identify experiences, relationships and environments where the child has felt safe and supported;
- assess current relationships to understand who the child trusts and why;
- recognise cultural, spiritual, or other meaningful connections that provide the child with a sense of safety and belonging.

Recognise the duality of power in ambivalence

By exploring both the positive and negative expressions of power a child has experienced, social workers should remain attentive to areas where the child may hold mixed or uncertain feelings about people or situations. To do this, social workers can:

- use open-ended, non-leading questions to gently explore situations or relationships that seem emotionally complex or uncertain for the child;
- listen for contradictions or hesitations in the child's narrative, which may suggest conflicting emotions;
- acknowledge and validate ambivalence as a normal and understandable response, especially in situations involving people the child may love, but who have also caused them harm.

Delivering empowering interventions

Based on the assessment, it is recommended that empowering interventions are planned and delivered, with a view to supporting children to develop a sense of agency and control in age-appropriate ways. Such interventions may help counteract the effects of past disempowerment while reinforcing the child's inherent strengths. The following suggestions outline ways in which children may be empowered through interventions.

Actively involve children in care and support planning

Rebuilding children's sense of power through participation is key to delivering empowering interventions. Once a child's experiences of power have been understood, social workers should empower children through support and care planning processes. Although some frameworks consider planning separately (Parker, 2020), it directly shapes interventions by determining the practical steps required to meet assessed needs. Engagement in the planning process is therefore considered part of the intervention phase from a power-informed perspective. To facilitate children's engagement within the planning process, social workers can:

- involve children in decision-making in age-appropriate ways wherever possible;
- offer children choices where appropriate;
- recognise when interventions feel forced and allow children to have as much say and control as possible; even when aspects of a necessary intervention may be restrictive, creative solutions can often be found.

Collaborate with children as participants in their support

Wherever possible, children should be engaged as active participants in their support rather than being treated as passive recipients. To support collaboration with children during ongoing interventions, social workers can:

- work alongside children on an ongoing basis in developmentally appropriate ways to respond to their needs;
- adapt interventions to reflect children's evolving understanding and input;
- regularly check in with children about how they feel the support is working and adjust plans based on their feedback.

Ensure children's voices are central to multiagency work

Social workers who recognise the significance of power in a child's experiences need to ensure children's voices remain at the forefront of multiagency work by:

- advocating on behalf of children by communicating their wishes and feelings to other professionals, such as those in education, healthcare and legal services;
- where necessary, challenging decisions that overlook or minimise the child's wishes and feelings, ensuring that their voice remains central, even when actions are justified as being in their 'best interests';
- advocating for power-informed responses to child abuse within other professional settings/contexts.

While direct work with children is essential in helping to restore a sense of power following experiences of abuse, it cannot occur independently of the wider systems that influence children's lives. Children's lives and experiences are inseparable from their family and community contexts (Lonne et al., 2016), which may either reinforce or challenge disempowerment. Therefore, PIP must also extend to how social workers engage with parents, families and communities, recognising both the potential for harm and the opportunities for empowerment within these relationships.

Working with parents, carers, families and communities

Lonne et al. (2016) argue that child protection practices should move beyond focusing solely on the child and acknowledge the broader impact on parents, grandparents and communities. They critique the dominant risk-based models that often narrowly concentrate on assessing child safety and identifying deficits. Instead, they advocate for relational, value-driven approaches that consider the wellbeing of the entire family system. This shift is seen to be particularly important because risk-focused models tend to disproportionately affect disadvantaged and marginalised communities.

The power-informed perspective supports this critique by emphasising how power is relational and contextual and is exercised on multiple levels to shape the experiences of individuals. Social workers should therefore engage not only with the child, but also, where appropriate, with the child's family and/or community. By doing so, they can work towards improving family functioning, addressing broader challenges and reducing the risk of future harm to the child. While the guidance in this chapter has focused on direct work with children, the critical role of the family in child protection efforts is also recognised. The following case study offers one example of how the PIP model and its principles may be applied to provide holistic support within the statutory child protection context.

Case study 8.1: Fariha

Background

Fariha, a 13-year-old girl of Somali heritage, lives in an inner-city area with her mother, Adena. Fariha's father died when she was six and, since then, her mother has relied heavily on support from male relatives, particularly her older brother, who has been staying at the house frequently over the past few years due to housing instability. Fariha's paternal grandmother, Amburo, lives nearby and occasionally helps with childcare. Adena finds it difficult to ask Amburo for help unless she has no other choice, as her presence evokes painful memories of her late husband and the life they all once shared.

Fariha was referred to children's social care by the school nurse when Fariha made a troubling disclosure about how 'something bad had happened at home', but would say no more. During an initial meeting with a duty social worker, Fariha shared that her uncle had entered her room on multiple occasions over the last year and had sexually abused her. Fariha also shared that he had recently left the UK to return to Somalia due to his immigration status, and so she had not told her mother about what had happened. A Section 47 enquiry was therefore initiated to assess current risk and offer support.

1. Establishing power-aware relationships

Fariha was allocated a female social worker named Sahar, who was conscious of the inherent power differences between herself as a professional authority figure and Fariha as a young, minoritised girl who had experienced sexual abuse in her own home (Principle 2). From the outset, therefore, Sahar focused on building a power-aware relationship grounded in empathy, consistency and cultural awareness. To support Fariha's sense of psychological safety, Sahar arranged for meetings to take place at school, where Fariha had said she felt safest. She also offered Fariha the option of having a support worker present if she wanted. Sahar recognised that power is shaped by relationships and contexts (Principle 1), she therefore endeavoured to create a supportive environment for Fariha. By being mindful of how power is present in action and inaction (Principle 3), Sahar also ensured she arrived for meetings when she said she would and followed up on promises.

2. Undertaking power-informed assessments

During the assessment phase, Sahar sought to understand Fariha's experiences within the broader system of her family and community. Alongside the assessment of risk and protective factors in Fariha's life, Sahar endeavoured to map how power was operating at different levels (Principle 2) and how it was impacting on Fariha and her mother

Adena (Principle 4). Adena initially avoided Sahar, fearing stigma in the community. However, Sahar explained that the social work intervention could also help Adena and support her with protecting Fariha from being exposed to harm in the future. An understanding of the dual impact of professional involvement enabled Adena to recognise that the benefits outweighed potential negative consequences. This allowed her to become an active participant in Fariha's protection plan, rather than a recipient of an enforced intervention.

Fariha's wishes and feelings remained central to the assessment process. Sahar used age-appropriate methods to allow Fariha to communicate her experiences and needs at her own pace. During this time, Fariha shared that, since her father's death, she and her mother had often depended on her uncle for support and protection. She also expressed uncertainty about what would happen since he was no longer around to help. Sahar recognised how these past experiences of loss and reliance on extended family continued to shape how Fariha and her mother viewed their current circumstances and levels of power (Principle 5). Sahar also explored the role of Amburo, Fariha's paternal grandmother, as a potential source of emotional and practical support. Although Adena had found it difficult to ask Amburo for help, Sahar recognised how strengthening this relationship could contribute to a more sustainable and culturally grounded support network.

3. **Delivering empowering interventions**

The child protection plan prioritised Fariha's safety while maintaining stability for her and Adena. Sahar understood that delivering empowering interventions in this situation required her to support both Fariha and Adena. Sahar therefore also arranged one-to-one sessions with Adena to explore how historical patterns of family dependence, particularly following the loss of Fariha's father, had shaped her reliance on her brother. This helped Adena reflect on her conflicted emotions about her brother, ultimately resulting in her decision to cut all ties with him. By recognising how past power influences present power (Principle 5), Sahar was able to support Adena to process the complexity of her situation.

Sahar took great care to ensure that the statutory process did not replicate feelings of powerlessness for either Fariha or her mother. She consistently emphasised their participation in decision-making, and ensured they were kept up to date with relevant information. Fariha was offered a female mentor through a Somali-led youth support organisation and referred to specialist services for therapeutic support. These interventions were offered as choices rather than imposed, allowing Fariha to engage with them on her own terms. To support Fariha in her day-to-day life, Sahar also arranged for her to have a trusted teacher at school who she could approach if she ever felt overwhelmed. This created space for Fariha to rebuild trust in adult relationships and feel safe.

Sahar also supported Adena by helping her access a local community organisation which offered advice and support to parents. Through the community organisation, Fariha's mother connected with other single mothers who shared similar experiences, which offered her a safe space to talk, reflect and receive advice without judgement. As she began to build her own support network and engage in activities outside the home, Adena realised she did not need to rely so heavily on male support in the way she had done in the past; challenging her earlier assumptions about the reduced power she felt

(Continued)

she had. As part of the intervention, Sahar also helped Adena and Amburo reconnect and strengthen their relationship. This enabled Adena and Amburo to offer each other support, while also allowing Amburo to take a more active role in Fariha's care, just as she had always wanted.

Over time, as safety and stability were established for Fariha, Sahar made a conscious effort to gradually shift decision-making power back to Adena in her role as Fariha's parent, recognising that power is contextual and relational (Principle 1). This involved a carefully managed process of stepping down statutory involvement, transitioning the case from a child protection plan to a child in need plan and eventually closing the case altogether. Sahar ensured that both Fariha and Adena remained informed, actively involved and supported throughout each stage of this de-escalation. By doing so, she aimed to reduce the reliance on professional intervention and promote empowerment, enabling Fariha and Adena to regain control over their own lives with greater confidence and autonomy.

Conclusion

Fariha's case demonstrates how power-informed child protection practice can be effectively delivered when relationships, assessments and interventions are approached both critically and reflexively. By embedding the five principles of PIP within the three dimensions of social work engagement, Sahar was able to safeguard Fariha while also addressing broader power dynamics. Rather than viewing statutory intervention as a purely controlling force, therefore, the case study illustrates how ethical, power-informed social work can be used as a mechanism for support and empowerment.

Summary

This chapter has examined how professional power operates across the child protection continuum in England and demonstrated how prevention, early help and statutory intervention each involve escalating levels of power. Ethical considerations, such as confidentiality, informed consent and prioritising the child's best interests, were then discussed, as was the importance of cultural perspectives in guiding social work practice. Through the child-focused application of the three-dimensional practice model, the chapter also offered strategies for developing power-aware relationships, undertaking power-informed assessments and delivering empowering interventions. Ultimately, the chapter highlights the importance of power-informed social work practice as a foundation for ethical and effective engagement with children who have experienced abuse.

9 Working with adult victims/survivors of child abuse

Introduction

The language we use to describe individuals who were abused during their childhood has significant power implications and is more complicated than it may seem. The term 'victim' has been critiqued as a mechanism of state power that can contribute to the oppression of individuals (Walklate, 2006), whereas the term 'survivor' is often considered more empowering as it is thought to convey resilience and the capacity to overcome adversity (Brennan, 2015). However, research shows that individual preferences vary, and people may refer to themselves as victims and survivors, depending on the experience they are communicating or the stage of their healing (Karim, 2020). Given this complexity, the term *victim/survivor* is used throughout this book to reflect the different ways in which people self-identify. It is also intended to provide a more inclusive way of recognising both the suffering experienced and the strength demonstrated by individuals.

Mirroring the previous chapter, this chapter offers a power-informed practice (PIP) perspective for social work with adult victims/survivors of historic child abuse, highlighting the importance of considering power throughout interventions. The chapter begins with a discussion on how adult social care legislation in the UK, particularly the Mental Capacity Act 2005 and the Care Act 2014, reflects a negotiated approach to power. The chapter then moves on to explore key ethical principles which should be adhered to when working with adults, including balancing autonomy and risk, and navigating capacity and consent. The chapter concludes by offering guidance on the application of the three-dimensional PIP model (introduced in Chapter 7) when working with adult victims/survivors of child abuse.

Adult social care and power

Within adult social care, the power dynamics between practitioners and service users differ considerably from those present in children and families' social work. In child protection contexts, professional authority typically increases incrementally as the perceived risk to children escalates (see Chapter 8); in contrast, adult social care operates on a fundamentally different basis. In adult social work, power dynamics between practitioners and service users are shaped through ongoing negotiations concerning consent, capacity and risk. Unlike the often directive nature of children's social work, power in adult services tends to be exercised in partnership with the individual, respecting their legal autonomy and right to make decisions about their own lives as an adult who has the capacity to do so. Mental capacity is always specific to the particular decision being made and must be assessed at the time the decision is needed. This is because a person may have capacity for some decisions but not others, and their ability can change over time. Therefore, as long as adults have the capacity to make specific decisions at specific times, even if such decisions are considered to be 'unwise', they are free to do so (Jenkinson and Chamberlain, 2019).

In England and Wales, adults are presumed to have capacity and legal autonomy under the Mental Capacity Act 2005, meaning interventions usually require the person's consent. The Care Act 2014 further reinforces that working with adults should be a collaborative process, where professionals cannot impose interventions unless the adult lacks mental capacity or poses a significant risk to themselves or others. In Scotland, the equivalent legislation includes the Adults with Incapacity (Scotland) Act 2000, which guides decision-making and interventions when an adult lacks the capacity to make decisions for themselves. Alongside this, the Adult Support and Protection (Scotland) Act 2007 establishes specific duties and powers to protect adults at risk of harm. In Northern Ireland, the Mental Capacity Act (Northern Ireland) 2016 and the policy on *Adult Safeguarding: Prevention and Protection in Partnership* (DHSSPS/DoJ, 2015) provide a comparable framework.

Essentially, the legal framework for adult safeguarding in the UK places significant emphasis on autonomy, consent and negotiated interventions. The Care Act 2014 (Sections 42–5) establishes the duty of local authorities to make enquiries where an adult with care and support needs may be at risk of abuse or neglect and is unable to protect themselves. Six key principles underpin adult safeguarding practice in England in light of the Care Act 2014; these are the principles of:

- *empowerment*: supporting and enabling individuals to make their own choices and provide informed consent;
- *prevention*: acting early to stop harm before it happens;
- *proportionality*: responding in the least restrictive and most appropriate way according to the level of risk;
- *protection*: providing help, advocacy and representation for those most at risk;
- *partnership*: creating local solutions by working together with communities, who play an active role in identifying, preventing and reporting abuse and neglect;
- *accountability*: ensuring openness, responsibility and clear reporting on the way in which safeguarding is carried out.

(DoHSC, 2023)

Often, within adult social care contexts, professional power is balanced against the wishes and rights of service users, with interventions typically occurring when consent is obtained. Statutory guidance relating to the Care Act refers to 'power' and 'empowerment' throughout, highlighting the central role of power in shaping adult social care practice (DoHSC, 2023). This emphasis reflects the commitment to ensuring that adults retain maximum control over decisions affecting their lives, while safeguarding mechanisms provide necessary protections when risks need to be addressed.

However, the presence of risk in itself does not trigger the same escalation of professional authority in adult social work as it does in child protection contexts. Even in cases where risk is present, adult safeguarding remains advisory and negotiated unless specific legal thresholds are crossed as the Care Act 2014 places great emphasis on individual self-determination and desired outcomes (Johnson and Boland, 2019). Social workers may only intervene without the consent of service users in situations where they lack capacity, or where there is a significant risk of harm present for themselves or others. Even then, legal frameworks require that such actions be proportionate, rights-based, and the least restrictive option available (Mental Capacity Act, 2005). This creates a distinctive practice environment in adult social work, where the level of professional power is determined and adjusted in relation to consent, capacity and risk over time.

Figure 9.1 reflects how social work power in adult social care is negotiated and contingent upon consent, which is informed by capacity and risk.

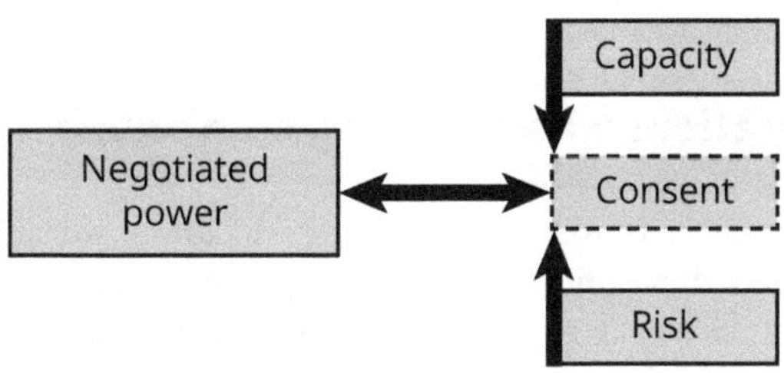

Figure 9.1 Social work power in adult social care

Case study 9.1

'Unwise' decisions

David is a 62-year-old male who lives alone at his home in a coastal town. He has a history of alcohol dependency and long-standing health conditions, including diabetes and limited mobility. David contacted his GP surgery to request a home visit following a fall. However, during his conversation with the secretary, he was adamant that he was 'managing just fine' and simply needed the doctor to check his injury at home. During the GP's home visit, David appeared to be under the influence of alcohol and there were visible signs of poor hygiene. The GP examined David and found that he had several wounds on his arms and legs which required treatment. The GP informed David of the treatment plan and also shared that he would be making a referral to adult social care for further support, despite David's resistance.

Following the referral to adult social care, a social worker visited David to assess the situation. During the conversation with the social worker, David was clear that he did not require services or any social work involvement. He acknowledged his alcohol use and health issues, but stated that he valued his independence and was content managing his life in his own way. David expressed frustration at what he described as people 'interfering' and insisted he would seek help if he felt he ever needed to.

During the visit, David also disclosed that he had experienced abuse when he was a child, sharing that he had a violent father and a mother who rarely paid any attention to him. He spoke about how these early experiences had affected his ability to trust people and that he had chosen to live alone and was comfortable with this decision, no matter what the consequences. David therefore demonstrated capacity to make decisions about his life and living arrangements, including an understanding of the potential risks involved.

The social worker was therefore faced with the challenge of balancing respect for David's autonomy and right to make unwise decisions, while considering the duty of care to safeguard his wellbeing.

Reflective questions

1. How much power does the social worker have in this scenario?
2. How can the social worker balance David's right to autonomy with their professional concerns about his wellbeing?
3. How might David's early experiences of power and abuse shape his response to professional intervention?

Ethical considerations when working with adults

When supporting adult victims/survivors of historic abuse, social workers must fulfil their ethical responsibilities, guided by the principles outlined in professional codes of practice (BASW, 2021; SWE, 2019). Ethical practice when working with adults requires balancing legal, professional and moral duties, particularly in relation to autonomy, consent, confidentiality and transparency. Unlike work with children, where practitioners are often required to intervene decisively in the child's best interests (Children Act 1989), adult social work places a stronger emphasis on respecting the individual's right to self-determination (Care Act 2014).

The long-term impacts of childhood abuse, including trauma, mistrust and feelings of powerlessness (Knight, 2015), can present additional challenges within the professional–client relationship. Social workers therefore have a crucial role to play in navigating ethical challenges with sensitivity, to help ensure that their interventions uphold the autonomy and rights of individuals, while providing appropriate protection and support.

Balancing autonomy and risk

> *Social workers should recognise that people using social work services have the right to take risks and should enable them to identify and manage potential and actual risk, while seeking to ensure that their behaviour does not harm themselves or other people. Social workers should support people to reach informed decisions about their lives and promote their autonomy and independence, provided this does not conflict with their safety or with the rights of others.*
>
> (BASW, 2021, Section 3.2)

Decision-making in adult social work often involves navigating complex situations where risk is present but does not automatically justify intervention. The BASW Code of Ethics (2021) highlights that adults have the right to make decisions about their own lives, including choices that may involve risk. For social workers, this means moving away from risk-averse or paternalistic approaches and, instead, supporting individuals to make informed choices while considering their safety and the safety of others. Balancing autonomy and protection requires careful, ethical judgement (Braye, Orr and Preston-Shoot, 2017), particularly when working with adult victim/survivors of childhood abuse, whose perceptions of acceptable levels of risk may be influenced by past experiences.

Navigating capacity and consent

Working collaboratively by offering agency and choice to victims/survivors is crucial to effective practice (Alyce et al., 2024). Respecting an individual's right to make decisions is a core ethical duty in adult social work when capacity is present, and this principle is firmly reinforced through legal frameworks (Mental Capacity Act 2005). Social workers must therefore recognise and uphold the autonomy of adults wherever possible, supporting them to make informed choices about their lives and care. However, situations can arise where an individual's capacity to make specific decisions is impaired. In such circumstances, the role of the social worker becomes even more critical to ensuring that their rights are protected and ethical standards are maintained. The *Knowledge and Skills Statement for Social Workers in Adult Services* (DoH, 2015) provides guidance on how capacity and consent should be navigated:

> *Social workers must understand their responsibilities for people who are assessed as lacking capacity at a particular time and must ensure that they are supported to be involved in decisions about themselves and their care as far as is possible. Where they are unable to be*

> *involved in the decision-making process, decisions should be taken in their best interests following consultation with all appropriate parties, including families and carers. Social workers must seek to ensure that an individual's care plan is the least restrictive possible to achieve the intended outcomes.*
>
> (p. 4)

Maintaining boundaries

Maintaining boundaries is crucial when working with adult service users. However, it is noted that adult victims/survivors of child abuse and professionals both face challenges in establishing and maintaining appropriate boundaries (Harper, 2006). Ethical standards for practice highlight that professionals hold power by virtue of their position, making professional boundaries critical. Crossing these boundaries constitutes a breach of trust and an abuse of authority. It is further explained that boundaries can be crossed through the giving and receiving of gifts, extending invitations to social events or meeting socially, developing friendships or personal relationships, borrowing or lending money, providing a service user with personal contact information, or connecting with them on social media (HCPC, 2025).

Confidentiality and information sharing

In adult social work, as in work with children and families, confidentiality is a core principle that underpins trust and respect in professional relationships (Millstein, 2000). However, confidentiality is not absolute. Under the Data Protection Act 2018, professionals are legally obliged to share information when a risk of harm to the individual or others is identified. Social workers must therefore carefully balance the right to confidentiality with their safeguarding duties, considering necessity, proportionality and the individual's consent wherever possible (SCIE, 2019). In situations where information is shared on a lawful basis without the consent of service users, individuals retain the legal right to know how information is being used (DPA, 2018). Social workers must therefore ensure that service users are appropriately informed about what information is being shared and for what purpose.

Transparency

Social workers are required to build relationships with adult service users that are grounded in openness, transparency and empathy (DoH, 2015). The experience of child abuse is often characterised by secrecy and betrayal, and experiences of historic abuse can significantly impact the ability of individuals to form trusting relationships (Alyce et al., 2024). To address this, decisions taken at both the individual and service levels should be open and transparent, with the aim of building trust and fostering a sense of safety (Sweeney and Taggart, 2019). Transparency is therefore not only an ethical responsibility, but also a necessary practice to support empowerment in social work with adult victims/survivors.

Activity 9.1: Professional boundaries

Isla is a registered social worker based in a rural town in the north of England. She works as a community wellbeing practitioner, supporting adults with mild to moderate mental health needs through outreach and short-term interventions. Due to the close-knit nature of the community, Isla frequently encounters service users in everyday settings such as the local post office, library and community centre.

One of her new clients, Callum, has been referred for support following a period of low mood and social withdrawal linked to work-related stress and family pressures. A few weeks into their sessions, Callum invites Isla to join a local walking group he is helping to organise. Isla enjoys walking and is keen to support community wellbeing, but she is worried that accepting the invitation could compromise professional boundaries.

Ethical dilemma

Isla must consider whether participating in the walking group would blur the lines of her professional relationship with Callum. While community engagement is encouraged in her role, she is concerned that she may breach ethical standards around maintaining boundaries with service users.

Reflective questions

1. How should Isla respond to the ethical dilemma?
2. What factors should be considered when balancing community involvement with professional responsibilities?
3. How might Isla's decision impact Callum's perception of their working relationship and her role as a social worker?

Power-informed practice: guidance for social workers supporting adult victims/survivors of abuse

Mirroring the approach for working with children (Chapter 8), the following guidance is not intended to be fixed, exhaustive, or prescriptive. Instead, it offers a foundation for developing PIP, which must remain flexible, responsive and tailored to the unique experiences and needs of every individual. Based on the principles of PIP and the three-dimensional practice model (Chapter 7), the guidance aims to support direct work with adult victims/survivors of abuse who are assessed to have the capacity to consent to interventions and are able to communicate their experiences, wishes and feelings. When working with adults with cognitive impairments, disabilities or other vulnerabilities, a power-informed perspective may be incorporated into the overall approach to ensure that individuals are supported in a way that aligns with their specific experiences and needs.

Social workers may engage with adult victims/survivors of historic child abuse within both statutory and non-statutory practice settings. In some cases, individuals may be engaging with local authority adult services due to their care and support needs, while in others they may be accessing health services, community organisations etc. In recognition of the diverse contexts in which social workers may interact with victims/survivors, therefore, the following guidance is intended to be flexible in its application within processes of establishing power-aware relationships, undertaking power-informed assessments and delivering empowering interventions.

Establishing power-aware relationships with victims/survivors

As adults, victims/survivors of abuse often carry the experiences of powerlessness over a prolonged period of time, which can result in deep-seated feelings of mistrust towards others (Fleming et al., 1999). These feelings may have been reinforced by repeated experiences of being dismissed or further harmed by professionals or organisations that were required to provide protection during their lives – that is, experiences of *institutional betrayal* (Smith and Freyd, 2014). Establishing power-aware relationships is therefore central to effectively working with adult victims/survivors of historic abuse and requires a recognition of past experiences of power, transparency and fostering trust through consistency and reliability.

Acknowledge the victim/survivor's past experiences of power and powerlessness

Social workers must recognise that child abuse is an expression of limiting power, which often has long-term consequences. As a result, adult victims/survivors may continue to feel disempowered and distrustful of others. Their past experiences with individuals who misused power against them may well influence how they respond to professionals, as previous experiences of power can shape present day interactions. Social workers therefore need to:

- acknowledge past experiences of power to demonstrate empathy and understanding;
- validate feelings and experiences by actively listening and making adjustments as appropriate;
- recognise that if victims/survivors appear to be withdrawn or resistant, these responses may stem from their past experiences of limiting expressions of power.

Adopt transparency as appropriate

While complete transparency may not always be appropriate due to ethical or legal obligations, social workers should strive to extend transparency beyond conventional practice when working with adult victims/survivors by:

- explaining their role and any statutory obligations that may potentially impact them;
- being honest about the limits of their authority and influence, including what decisions they can and cannot make;
- being transparent about confidentiality, its limits and information sharing.

Foster trust through consistency and reliability

As with children, building trust with adult victims/survivors of child abuse requires social workers to demonstrate consistency and reliability. Victims/survivors may have experienced betrayal throughout their lives and such histories require social workers to maintain a consistent approach in their engagement. A consistent approach helps create a sense of safety and predictability – critical to building a trusting relationship. To foster trust through consistency and reliability, social workers should:

- follow through on commitments to avoid creating limiting experiences of power for individuals as a result of inaction;
- regularly check in and meet with individuals to provide consistent support;
- provide regular updates about the actions which are being undertaken on their behalf and remove uncertainty wherever possible.

Undertaking power-informed assessments

Effective assessments with adult victims/survivors of child abuse must go beyond identifying immediate needs or presenting concerns. They should reflect a nuanced understanding of how power has operated throughout the individual's life, through personal relationships to professional interactions and broader social/structural influences. Social workers are encouraged to consider how these intersecting dimensions have shaped the adult's experiences holistically. The following guidance outlines practical approaches to help explore these layers of power and their impact within the assessment process.

Recognise how power operates at multiple levels

For the purposes of assessment, it is important for social workers to recognise the different levels at which power has been and is being exercised to impact victims/survivors. As part of the assessment process, social workers should consider the following:

- *individual/personal power*: exploring how power has been experienced within close relationships across the life course, including those with family members, partners, peers and others;
- *professional/institutional power*: reflecting on how interactions with education, health and other professional systems have shaped the victim/survivor's experiences, while remaining mindful of how social work involvement is also being experienced by them;
- *structural/societal power*: recognising how broader social forces, such as legal systems, cultural norms, economic inequality and discrimination, may have influenced the victim/survivor's life and sense of agency. These structural power dynamics may have contributed to the original abuse, shaped responses to it, or affected access to support and justice.

Explore how power has been used in limiting ways

As part of the assessment process, exploring how power has been used in limiting ways against individuals can help to identify what made them feel powerless and how. In practice, this means that social workers must be skilled in assessing the power dynamics that have affected the individual across their life course and understand how these dynamics may continue to contribute to feelings of powerlessness. Social workers can begin to map and assess an adult's experiences of limiting power by:

- engaging with individuals using approaches that support safe and open communication (e.g., open-ended questions, reflective listening, or creative expression, where appropriate);
- exploring situations where the individual may have felt powerless, including within family relationships, professional interactions, or community contexts;
- considering individual experiences of limiting power related to broader factors such as ethnicity, socioeconomic status, gender and disability within assessments.

Explore how power has been used in productive ways

Alongside the limiting expressions of power, it is equally important to recognise that individuals will have experienced positive expressions of power during their lives. Social workers can begin to assess this by:

- identifying experiences, relationships and environments where the individual has felt supported or empowered;
- exploring current and past relationships to understand who the individual trusts and why;
- recognising cultural, spiritual or other connections that provide the victim/survivor with a sense of safety and belonging.

Recognise the duality of power in ambivalence

As part of the assessment, it is important to recognise that adult victims/survivors may hold mixed or ambivalent feelings about particular people or life experiences. Such experiences often include both positive and negative expressions of power, which can leave individuals with conflicted emotions or uncertainties. To assess ambivalence which may have resulted from the dual impact of power, social workers can:

- use open-ended, non-leading questions to gently explore relationships or experiences that seem emotionally complex;
- listen for contradictions, hesitations, or shifts in the individual's narrative that may reflect conflicting emotions or unresolved feelings;
- acknowledge and validate ambivalence as a normal and understandable response, particularly in relationships or experiences that have been both positive and negative.

Delivering empowering interventions

Based on the assessment, it is recommended that empowering interventions are planned and delivered, with a view to enhancing an individual's sense of agency and power. Such interventions may help counteract the effects of past disempowerment while reinforcing the individual's inherent strengths. The following suggestions outline some of the ways in which victims/survivors may be empowered through interventions.

Actively involve victims/survivors in shaping their support and care plans

Support and care planning should be participatory processes that place victims/survivors at the centre of decision-making wherever possible. As mentioned previously, although some frameworks consider planning separately (Parker, 2020), it directly shapes interventions by determining the steps required to meet assessed needs. Service-user engagement within the planning process is therefore considered part of the intervention phase from a power-informed perspective. Social workers must support individuals to take on an active role in such processes to ensure that proposed interventions align with their needs. To support this, social workers should:

- facilitate victim/survivor-led decision-making when determining interventions;
- offer options rather than single pathways for support, ensuring that victims/survivors have a say in the nature and timing of interventions; this may also include referrals for specialist support;
- recognise that interventions may sometimes feel restrictive (e.g., statutory involvement) and consider ways to maximise autonomy within these constraints as far as possible.

Collaborate with victims/survivors as partners in their support

Promoting agency through ongoing collaboration is central to delivering empowering interventions. Victim/survivors should therefore be engaged as equal partners throughout their support, rather than solely treated as passive recipients of services. To facilitate collaboration through interventions, social workers can:

- tailor support to align with the self-identified priorities of individuals;
- work alongside individuals on an ongoing basis to ensure interventions are responsive to their needs;
- actively seek feedback from individuals and adjust interventions accordingly;
- promote personal ownership and long-term empowerment throughout the intervention process.

Ensure victim/survivor voices are central to multiagency working

Social workers who recognise the role of power in shaping individual experiences must advocate for victim/survivor-centred, power-informed approaches across professional networks by:

- ensuring victim/survivor perspectives inform decisions made within multiagency contexts (e.g., with health, housing, etc.);
- challenging policies and practices that may disempower victims/survivors, such as service exclusion criteria that may limit access to support;
- advocating for power-informed responses to historic child abuse across professional contexts/settings.

Case study 9.2

Historic abuse and professional power in adult social work

Elaine is a 55-year-old woman who spent most of her childhood in residential homes during the 1970s and early 1980s, after being removed from her family home due to severe neglect. While in care, she endured repeated physical punishment and inconsistent caregiving, which contributed to long-term post-traumatic stress and chronic musculoskeletal pain. Now living alone in social housing with limited family contact, Elaine reached out to adult social services when her physical health declined to the point where she was struggling with basic daily tasks, such as maintaining her hygiene, getting dressed and preparing meals. Although Elaine recognised that she should have made contact sooner, her deep-seated mistrust of authority figures had prevented her from doing so (Principle 5) until she felt she had no other choice.

1. **Establishing power-aware relationships**

Elaine's allocated social worker, Fiona, was acutely aware of the profound power imbalances rooted in Elaine's childhood experiences of both familial and institutional abuse. She recognised that power is contextual and relational (Principle 1) and that it operates across multiple levels, including the professional/institutional level (Principle 2), which she herself represented. In response, Fiona worked collaboratively with Elaine, moving at her pace to build trust gradually.

Whenever possible, Fiona arranged to meet Elaine in her own home rather than in unfamiliar office settings, recognising the importance of comfort and familiarity. She was consistently punctual, honoured her commitments and maintained transparency about her professional role and legal obligations. In conversations with Elaine, Fiona openly acknowledged the poor practices that were prevalent in residential care during the 1970s and 1980s. She invited Elaine to share her experiences if she felt comfortable doing so, and responded with empathy by validating her feelings and showing that her experiences were heard and taken seriously. Understanding that Elaine's past experiences shaped her current perceptions of control and autonomy (Principle 5), Fiona actively involved her in decisions about how the assessment should be carried out. By offering meaningful choices, Fiona began to shift power back to Elaine, fostering a more equitable relationship.

2. **Undertaking power-informed assessments**

In addition to assessing Elaine's current needs, Fiona carried out a power-informed assessment that traced how power dynamics had shaped Elaine's life experiences. The assessment considered power across three interconnected levels:

- **micro-level (individual/personal power)**: Fiona examined how Elaine's ability to express her needs had been suppressed by her previous experiences of limiting exercises of power. These experiences had contributed to a diminished sense of agency and self-worth. Fiona therefore ensured Elaine's views were central to the assessment – shaping its focus around her expressed needs and priorities;
- **meso-level (professional/institutional power)**: the assessment explored Elaine's engagement with professionals and institutions, including healthcare and housing.

Fiona identified incidences of professional neglect, including a counselling referral initiated by Elaine's GP that was never acted upon – that is, no contact was made by the service, which had deepened Elaine's mistrust of professionals (Principle 3). These experiences were contrasted with more positive expressions of professional power, such as when a housing officer assessed Elaine's accessibility needs and advocated for her to be moved to more suitable accommodation;

- **macro-level (structural/societal power)**: Fiona also considered the structural/societal level of power and how it had been experienced by Elaine. Fiona recognised the shifts in child and adult social care legislation, and the changes in social attitudes towards child abuse over the years. Elaine shared how these broader factors had shaped her experiences of disclosure, access to support and the responses she received from professionals.

Throughout the assessment, Fiona remained sensitive to the ambivalence present when the impact of power is simultaneously limiting and productive (Principle 4). For instance, Elaine recalled being removed from her home and placed in care as a child; a memory that evoked mixed emotions about whether the intervention had helped or not. Elaine explained that the severe punishment she received while in care was largely a response to her challenging behaviour, which stemmed from her frustration about being forcefully separated from her mother. Fiona validated these conflicting feelings, acknowledging that removing children from their parents can often carry both harm and benefit, and that Elaine's feelings were justified and understandable.

3. **Delivering empowering interventions**

Drawing on the assessment, Fiona co-produced a care and support plan in partnership with Elaine. Rather than prescribing a single model of home care, Fiona and Elaine explored two tailored options: daily visits from a care worker to assist with personal hygiene and meals, or receiving direct payments to arrange and pay for her own carers. Elaine chose the direct payments option, valuing the flexibility and control it gave her over who provided her support and when.

As Elaine became more confident, Fiona arranged to reduce her own involvement, moving from weekly check-ins to fortnightly, then monthly reviews, gradually shifting decision-making power firmly back to Elaine. During this time, Elaine expressed a wish to retrieve her care records and asked Fiona for help. Although this was not explicitly part of Fiona's professional role, she recognised the trust that Elaine was placing in her. She therefore extended her involvement and proactively supported Elaine to access her records and access further support via a referral to a victim/survivor support organisation.

Conclusion

The case study illustrates how the power-informed perspective can support practitioners in adult social work settings to consciously engage with power and promote genuine empowerment. By establishing power-aware relationships, conducting power-informed assessments and co-producing empowering interventions, Fiona supported Elaine in reclaiming agency over her health and wellbeing. Rather than perpetuating cycles of disempowerment, the approach demonstrates how social work can begin to work in power-informed ways to meet presenting needs and address the legacy of historic abuse.

Summary

This chapter began by exploring power in adult social work contexts, particularly in light of the Mental Capacity Act 2005 and the Care Act 2014, emphasising how they promote a negotiated model of professional power grounded in notions of service-user autonomy, consent and collaboration. In doing so, it highlighted the stark contrast between adult and children's social work, demonstrating how the level of power in adult social work practice is determined by consent, capacity and levels of risk, as opposed to the escalation of power based on safeguarding thresholds and the legal duty to protect children from harm in child protection contexts.

Building on this foundation, the chapter explored key ethical principles in relation to working with adults, before introducing PIP guidance for direct work with adult victims/survivors of abuse. Based on the three-dimensional model for practice (which was introduced earlier), the guidance focused on establishing power-aware relationships, undertaking power-informed assessments and delivering empowering interventions, to demonstrate how social workers can embed power-awareness into their practice. Ultimately, the chapter urges professionals to consciously share power with adult victims/survivors of historic abuse and use this as a foundation for sustainable, long-term solutions that challenge and address the limiting effects of past experiences of power and disempowerment.

Conclusion

Power is ever-present, yet it often remains unspoken, unexamined, and misunderstood. This book began with a call to confront and understand power so that it could be used ethically and intentionally to inform social work practice. Throughout the book, readers have been invited to reflect, question, and engage, as power is not something we can afford to ignore; not in our systems, our practice, or within ourselves. While examining power is essential across all areas of social work, this text has highlighted how critical it is in the context of child abuse, as abuse represents a limiting and harmful exercise of power.

Chapter 1 introduced child abuse as a global concern, which can be influenced by cultural practices, economic inequalities, and intersecting social identities. The chapter also examined international frameworks like the UN Convention on the Rights of the Child (UNCRC) and Sustainable Development Goals (SDGs), noting their importance in setting global standards while recognising the need for localised, context-specific implementation.

Chapter 2 focused on the UK policy context, tracing the evolution of child protection legislation and expanding definitions of child abuse over time. It also explored the concept of historic abuse and its definitions. The chapter emphasised the importance of integrating new knowledge into practice, while acknowledging ongoing challenges present in responding to past and present harm.

Chapter 3 provided an overview of recognised forms of child abuse, including physical, sexual, emotional/psychological abuse, neglect, child sexual exploitation (CSE), fabricated or induced illness (FII), and female genital mutilation (FGM). It also examined the growing role of technology in enabling harm, highlighting risks such as online grooming and AI-generated abuse materials. The chapter stressed the need for practitioners to remain critically reflective and responsive to emerging threats to children in a constantly shifting social and digital landscape.

Chapter 4 explored both the immediate and longer-term impacts of abuse on children and adults, highlighting its potential effects on individuals and their lives. The chapter also addressed societal implications, reinforcing the need to work collectively to address the issue, as child protection is everyone's responsibility.

Chapter 5 focused on perpetrators, by presenting demographic data and considering psychological and sociological explanations for abusive behaviour. It also highlighted the misuse of power by professionals in positions of authority in the context of institutional abuse and challenged deterministic views of the victim-to-perpetrator cycle. In doing so, it cautions against simplistic narratives, as perpetrating child abuse is not an inevitable outcome of histories of abuse.

Chapter 6 revisited the concept of power, drawing on sociological and social work theory to explore its complexity and contested nature. It introduced the Power-Informed Practice (PiP) framework to simplify and conceptualise power as operating across three interconnected levels: individual/personal (I), professional/institutional (P), and structural/

societal (S). The chapter also emphasised the need to recognise how power is expressed through action and inaction, which can impact in limiting, productive and simultaneously limiting/productive ways.

Chapter 7 built on the PiP framework, outlining five principles for power-informed social work. It demonstrated how a power-informed perspective can enhance existing approaches, but can also be used as a stand-alone model for practice, through its recognition of the importance of establishing power-aware relationships, undertaking power-informed assessments and delivering empowering interventions.

Chapter 8 began by demonstrating how professional power increases across the child protection continuum, from prevention and early help to statutory intervention, while also considering the ethical dimensions of working with children. The chapter went on to apply the power-informed principles and practice model to direct work with child victims of abuse, and offered strategies for building relationships, conducting assessments, and delivering interventions.

Chapter 9 considered the role of legislation, which informs a negotiated framework of professional power in adult social care contexts which is based on consent, capacity and risk. The chapter also highlighted ethical considerations when working with adults and extended the application of the power-informed principles and practice model to direct work with adult victims/survivors of historic abuse.

Throughout the book, the theme of power has been central. Power is contextual and relational and is understood to be exercised on three levels. Further, power is realised through action and inaction, it has limiting, productive, or simultaneously limiting/productive impacts, and previous experiences of power can influence the present. It is hoped that such insights have made power more accessible for social workers, who can now begin to engage with it more confidently in practice. However, this is not the end of the conversation on power; it is only the beginning. If power shapes the world, then engaging with it continuously is not optional—it is essential. This book is an invitation to that ongoing journey: to see power clearly, to use it ethically, and to challenge it when it causes harm, so that we can imagine a world where everyone is truly safe.

But how can we respond in situations where we feel we have no power? There is a well-known piece of wisdom that speaks to the layered response to wrongdoing: If you witness wrongdoing, change it with your hands; if you are unable to do that, then speak out against it; and if even that is not possible, then reject it in your heart. This principle reflects the reality of social justice, where individuals may not always be able to intervene directly, but must still remain ethically engaged with the impact of power, even when it does not affect them personally. It reminds us that power is exercised not only through our actions, but also through what we choose to ignore or allow. Silence, inaction, and avoidance are not neutral; they are expressions of power too. And if we are accountable for what we do, then we are equally accountable for what we choose not to do. Yet in recognising our responsibility, we also reclaim our power: to choose compassion, to use power with integrity, and to increase our efforts in creating a better world.

Appendix

Professional Capabilities Framework

The 9 Domains

1. PROFESSIONALISM – Identify and behave as a professional social worker, committed to professional development
2. VALUES AND ETHICS – Apply social work ethical principles and values to guide professional practices
3. DIVERSITY AND EQUALITY – Recognise diversity and apply anti-discriminatory and anti-oppressive principles in practice
4. RIGHTS, JUSTICE AND ECONOMIC WELLBEING – Advance human rights and promote social justice and economic wellbeing
5. KNOWLEDGE – Develop and apply relevant knowledge from social work practice and research, social sciences, law, other professional and relevant fields, and from the experience of people who use services
6. CRITICAL REFLECTION AND ANALYSIS – Apply critical reflection and analysis to inform and provide a rationale for professional decision-making

7. SKILLS AND INTERVENTIONS – Use judgement, knowledge and authority to intervene with individuals, families and communities to promote independence, provide support, prevent harm and enable progress
8. CONTEXTS AND ORGANISATIONS – Engage with, inform, and adapt to changing organisational contexts, and the social and policy environments that shape practice. Operate effectively within and contribute to the development of organisations and services, including multi-agency and inter-professional settings.
9. PROFESSIONAL LEADERSHIP – Promote the profession and good social work practice. Take responsibility for the professional learning and development of others. Develop personal influence and be part of the collective leadership and impact of the profession.

Published with kind permission of BASW (www.basw.co.uk)

PCF chapter list

1: The global challenge of child abuse

This chapter will help you develop the following capabilities from the PCF.

Professionalism

This chapter encourages social workers to engage with global perspectives on child abuse, fostering a professional commitment to continuous learning and ethical practice.

Values and ethics

By challenging assumptions and highlighting systemic issues, the chapter helps social workers reflect on their own values and consider ethics.

Diversity

The exploration of cultural practices and intersecting social identities enhances social workers' understanding of diversity. It supports cultural awareness and helps practitioners recognise how different contexts shape children's experiences.

Rights, justice and economic wellbeing

The chapter deepens understanding of children's rights through the UNCRC and SDGs, helping social workers advocate for justice and economic wellbeing. It reinforces the importance of rights-based approaches in child protection.

Knowledge

By engaging with international frameworks and research, the chapter equips social workers with evidence-informed knowledge. It encourages critical engagement with global and local perspectives on child maltreatment.

Critical reflection and analysis

The nuanced discussion of abuse-related factors promotes reflective thinking. Social workers are supported to analyse complex issues.

Intervention and skills

Although not focused on direct practice, the chapter encourages the development of contextually informed interventions. It helps social workers consider how global standards can be adapted to local realities in safeguarding work.

Contexts and organisations

The chapter situates child protection within international and national policy frameworks, helping social workers understand the organisational and systemic contexts that shape practice.

Professional leadership

By engaging with global goals and advocating for systemic change, the chapter inspires social workers to take leadership roles in promoting child rights and influencing policy.

2: Child abuse and the UK policy context

This chapter will help you develop the following capabilities from the PCF.

Professionalism

This chapter supports professional development by encouraging social workers to understand the historical and evolving nature of child protection legislation. It reinforces the importance of staying informed about legal changes and integrating new knowledge into practice.

Values and ethics

By highlighting shifts in legal thinking and the recognition of indirect and historic abuse, the chapter helps social workers reflect on ethical responsibilities when working with individuals affected by abuse.

Diversity

The chapter touches on how evolving definitions of abuse reflect changing social attitudes and new understandings. This supports awareness of diverse experiences and the need for inclusive, responsive practice.

Rights, justice and economic wellbeing

The focus on children's rights and the recognition of historic abuse aligns with justice-oriented practice. It encourages social workers to advocate for those whose experiences were previously dismissed or ignored.

Knowledge

By tracing the development of legislation and definitions of abuse, the chapter provides a strong foundation of legal and historical knowledge.

Critical reflection and analysis

The chapter encourages reflection on how societal attitudes and legal frameworks shape definitions of harm. It supports critical analysis of past and present approaches to child protection.

Contexts and organisations

The chapter situates child protection within the legal and institutional context of the UK, helping social workers understand how organisational responses have changed over time and the implications for current practice.

3: Forms of child abuse

This chapter will help you develop the following capabilities from the PCF.

Professionalism

This chapter supports professional development by encouraging social workers to stay informed on the forms of abuse. It reinforces the importance of adapting practice to reflect current risks, including those posed by digital technologies.

Values and ethics

By emphasising the power imbalances underlying abuse and the implications of emerging forms of harm, the chapter helps social workers reflect on their responsibilities to protect children in evolving contexts.

Diversity

The chapter acknowledges the varied experiences of abuse, including culturally specific harms such as FGM, supporting an awareness of how abuse manifests differently across contexts.

Rights, justice and economic wellbeing

The discussion on legal responses, such as the Online Safety Act 2023, highlights the role of policy in protecting children's rights. It encourages social workers to advocate for justice in both physical and digital environments.

Knowledge

By outlining definitions, indicators and legal frameworks, the chapter provides essential knowledge for recognising and responding to different forms of abuse.

Critical reflection and analysis

The chapter encourages reflection on how abuse evolves and intersects with technology. It supports critical thinking about safeguarding in complex and rapidly changing social and digital landscapes.

Intervention and skills

The detailed overview of abuse types and indicators helps social workers develop practical skills in assessment and intervention. It promotes informed responses to both traditional and emerging safeguarding concerns.

4: The impact of child abuse

This chapter will help you develop the following capabilities from the PCF.

Professionalism

This chapter supports professional development by encouraging social workers to understand the wide-ranging impact of child abuse.

Values and ethics

By highlighting the immediate and long-term consequences of child maltreatment, the chapter helps social workers reflect on their ethical duty to advocate for victims/survivors and prevent future harm.

Diversity

The chapter acknowledges that the impact of abuse varies for individuals in both the immediate and longer term. It supports awareness of how personal, relational and social factors shape experiences and outcomes.

Rights, justice and economic wellbeing

The discussion on the potential long-term impact on economic stability for adult victims/survivors highlights the need for social workers to consider long-term wellbeing in their interventions.

Knowledge

By outlining the physical, psychological, developmental and societal effects of abuse, the chapter provides essential knowledge for understanding the full scope of harm to support holistic practice.

Critical reflection and analysis

The chapter encourages reflection on how abuse affects individuals and society over time. It supports critical thinking about the role of power and the need for systemic responses to address child abuse.

Intervention and skills

The emphasis on power-informed interventions helps social workers consider how to respond effectively to both individual and societal consequences of abuse. It supports the development of thoughtful, context-sensitive practice.

Contexts and organisations

By examining the societal and economic impact of abuse, the chapter reinforces the need for coordinated responses from organisations.

5: Perpetrators of child abuse

This chapter will help you develop the following capabilities from the PCF.

Professionalism

This chapter supports professional development by encouraging social workers to engage critically with the complexities of perpetrator behaviour.

Values and ethics

By challenging simplistic narratives and promoting nuanced understanding of perpetrators, the chapter helps social workers reflect on ethical responsibilities around accountability and the protection of vulnerable children.

Diversity

The chapter highlights demographic patterns and dispels myths around ethnicity and offending, supporting non-discriminatory practice. It encourages awareness of how abuse manifests across different social contexts.

Knowledge

By exploring psychological and sociological theories, demographic data and patterns of offending, the chapter provides foundational knowledge for understanding perpetrator behaviour. It supports evidence-informed safeguarding practice.

Critical reflection and analysis

The chapter encourages critical thinking about the causes and contexts of abuse, including the intergenerational transmission of harm. It supports reflective analysis of complex safeguarding issues.

Contexts and organisations

The discussion of institutional abuse and professional perpetrators helps social workers understand how organisational cultures and structures can enable harm. It reinforces the need for accountability within systems.

6: Revisiting power and power frameworks

This chapter will help you develop the following capabilities from the PCF.

Professionalism

This chapter supports professional development by encouraging social workers to engage with theoretical frameworks that deepen their understanding of power.

Values and ethics

By exploring empowerment and anti-oppressive practice, the chapter helps social workers reflect on ethical principles and the responsible use of power in their interactions with service users.

Diversity

The chapter highlights how power operates differently across contexts, supporting awareness of diverse experiences and the need to recognise intersecting forms of disadvantage and privilege.

Rights, justice and economic wellbeing

The PIP framework's emphasis on structural/societal power encourages social workers to consider how systemic inequalities affect wellbeing and access to resources.

Knowledge

By exploring and critiquing power frameworks and introducing PIP, the chapter provides theoretical knowledge that supports critical engagement with core concepts in social work and aims to enhance understandings of how power shapes practice.

Critical reflection and analysis

The chapter promotes reflective thinking about how power is expressed and experienced. It supports analysis of past and present influences and encourages practitioners to examine their own position of power.

Contexts and organisations

By examining how power operates across the individual/personal, professional/institutional and structural/societal domains, the chapter helps social workers understand the contexts that shape their practice.

Professional leadership

The chapter encourages social workers to take leadership in promoting power-informed approaches to practice.

7: Power-informed practice for social work

This chapter will help you develop the following capabilities from the PCF.

Professionalism

This chapter contributes to professional development by supporting social workers to adopt a power-informed approach. It reinforces the importance of reflective, principled practice that responds to the realities of working within complex systems.

Values and ethics

By promoting empowerment and challenging oppression, the chapter helps social workers reflect on ethical responsibilities.

Diversity

The chapter acknowledges how professional power intersects with social identities such as gender and ethnicity. It supports inclusive practice by encouraging awareness of how power operates differently across diverse identities.

Rights, justice and economic wellbeing

The PIP approach supports rights-based practice by helping social workers recognise structural inequalities. It encourages interventions that promote justice and wellbeing for individuals and communities.

Knowledge

By outlining the principles of PIP and its application in practice, the chapter provides conceptual and practical knowledge. It supports critical engagement with power as a central theme in social work.

Critical reflection and analysis

The chapter encourages reflection on the limits and possibilities of professional power. It supports analytical thinking about how power influences relationships, assessments and interventions.

Intervention and skills

The PIP framework offers practical guidance for building power-aware relationships, conducting assessments and delivering empowering interventions. It supports skill development in ethically grounded and context-sensitive practice.

Contexts and organisations

By recognising the constraints of wider systems and introducing the idea of power-informed supervision, the chapter helps social workers understand the organisational context of their work and the importance of supportive structures.

Professional leadership

The chapter encourages social workers to lead change by adopting and promoting power-informed approaches. It supports leadership in challenging limiting uses of power and fostering empowerment across practice settings.

8: Working with child victims of abuse

This chapter will help you develop the following capabilities from the PCF.

Professionalism

This chapter supports professional development by encouraging social workers to understand how professional power operates across the child protection continuum. It reinforces the importance of ethical, reflective and responsive practice when working with children.

Values and ethics

By addressing confidentiality, informed consent and the child's best interests, the chapter helps social workers reflect on ethical principles. It supports values-led practice that prioritises the rights and wellbeing of children.

Diversity

The inclusion of cultural perspectives supports awareness of how the experiences and needs of individuals vary across contexts.

Rights, justice and economic wellbeing

The chapter reinforces the importance of protecting children's rights through ethical engagement and appropriate intervention.

Knowledge

By applying the three-dimensional practice model and outlining strategies for power-informed engagement, the chapter provides practical and theoretical knowledge to promote effective child protection.

Critical reflection and analysis

The chapter encourages reflection on how power escalates across different stages of child protection. It supports critical thinking about the role of the practitioner and the ethical implications of intervention.

Intervention and skills

The chapter offers strategies for building power-aware relationships, conducting assessments and delivering empowering interventions. It supports skill development in child-centred and ethically grounded practice.

Contexts and organisations

By situating practice within the child protection continuum in England, the chapter helps social workers understand the organisational and systemic contexts that shape their work with children.

Professional leadership

The chapter encourages social workers to lead in developing and promoting power-informed approaches to practice.

9: Working with adult victims/survivors of abuse

This chapter will help you develop the following capabilities from the PCF.

Professionalism

This chapter supports professional development by encouraging social workers to adopt a power-informed approach when working with adult victims/survivors. It reinforces the importance of reflective, collaborative practice grounded in legal frameworks and ethical engagement.

Values and ethics

By emphasising autonomy, consent and the impact of past disempowerment, the chapter helps social workers reflect on ethical responsibilities. It supports values-led practice that prioritises empowerment and long-term wellbeing.

Diversity

The chapter acknowledges how professional power intersects with individuals in practice contexts. It supports inclusive practice by encouraging sensitivity to the diverse experiences of adult victims/survivors.

Rights, justice and economic wellbeing

By grounding practice in the Mental Capacity Act and Care Act, the chapter reinforces the importance of upholding individual rights, through its recognition of how power is negotiated in adult social work contexts.

Knowledge

The chapter provides practical and theoretical knowledge through the application of the three-dimensional model. It supports understanding of how power operates in adult social work and promotes power-informed engagement with victims/survivors.

Critical reflection and analysis

The chapter encourages reflection on the contrast between adult and child protection frameworks. It supports critical thinking about how power, consent and capacity shape social work roles and responsibilities in adult social work.

Intervention and skills

By offering guidance on power-aware relationships, power-informed assessments and empowering interventions, the chapter supports skill development in PIP with adult victims/survivors.

Contexts and organisations

The chapter situates adult safeguarding within legal and organisational frameworks, helping social workers understand the systems that shape their practice and the limits of professional power.

Professional leadership

The chapter encourages social workers to lead in adopting power-informed approaches. It supports leadership in promoting sustainable, empowering solutions for adult survivors and advocating for systemic change.

References

Adams, R. (2017) *Empowerment, Participation and Social Work.* 4th edn. London: Red Globe Press.

Adoption and Children Act 2002. Available at: www.legislation.gov.uk/ukpga/2002/38/contents

Adult Support and Protection (Scotland) Act 2007. Available at: www.legislation.gov.uk/asp/2007/10/contents

Adults with Incapacity (Scotland) Act 2000. Available at: www.legislation.gov.uk/asp/2000/4/contents/enacted

Afifi, T.O., Sareen, J., Fortier, J., Taillieu, T., Turner, S., Cheung, K. and Henriksen, C.A. (2017) Child maltreatment and eating disorders among men and women in adulthood: results from a nationally representative United States sample. *International Journal of Eating Disorders*, 50(11), 1281–96. https://doi.org/10.1002/eat.22783

Akilapa, R. and Simkiss, D. (2012) Cultural influences and safeguarding children. *Paediatrics and Child Health*, 22(11), 490–5. https://doi.org/10.1016/j.paed.2012.06.008.

Aldgate, J. and Hill, M. (1995) Child welfare in the United Kingdom. *Children and Youth Services Review*, 17(5–6), 575–97.

Allegri, E., Rosina, B. and Sanfelici, M. (2022) Remaking social work by applying an anti-oppressive lens. In N.T. Tan and P. Shajahan (eds), *Remaking Social Work for the New Global Era.* Cham: Springer. https://doi.org/10.1007/978-3-031-08352-5_3

Alyce, S., Taggart, D. and Turton, J. (2024) Trust, entrusting and the role of trustworthiness for adult survivors of child sexual abuse. *Journal of Mental Health*, 1–10. https://doi.org/10.1080/09638237.2024.2390366

Anderson, C., John, O.P. and Keltner, D. (2012) The personal sense of power. *Journal of Personality*, 80(2), 313–44. https://doi.org/10.1111/j.1467-6494.2011.00734.x

Angelakis, I., Austin, J.L. and Gooding, P. (2020) Association of childhood maltreatment with suicide behaviors among young people: a systematic review and meta-analysis. *JAMA Network Open*, 3(8), e2012563. doi:10.1001/jamanetworkopen.2020.12563

Angelakis, I., Gillespie, E.L. and Panagioti, M. (2019) Childhood maltreatment and adult suicidality: a comprehensive systematic review with meta-analysis. *Psychological Medicine*, 49(7), 1057–78. doi: 10.1017/s0033291718003823. PMID: 30608046; PMCID: PMC6498789.

Arnot, M.L. (1994) Infant death, child care and the state: the baby-farming scandal and the first infant life protection legislation of 1872. *Continuity and Change*, 9(2), 271–311. doi:10.1017/S0268416000002290

Augarde, S. and Rydon-Grange, M. (2022) Female perpetrators of child sexual abuse: a review of the clinical and empirical literature – a 20-year update. *Aggression and Violent Behavior*, 62. https://doi.org/10.1016/j.avb.2021.101687

Avelino, F. (2021) Theories of power and social change: power contestations and their implications for research on social change and innovation. *Journal of Political Power*, 14(3), 425-48. doi: 10.1080/2158379X.2021.1875307

Bahk, Y.C., Jang, S.K., Choi, K.H. and Lee, S.H. (2017) The relationship between childhood trauma and suicidal ideation: role of maltreatment and potential mediators. *Psychiatry Investigation*, 14(1), 37–43. https://doi.org/10.4306/pi.2017.14.1.37

Bailey, R. and Brake, M. (eds) (1975) *Radical Social Work.* London: Edward Arnold.

Bar-On, A. (2002) Restoring power to social work practice. *British Journal of Social Work*, 32(8), 997–1014. https://doi.org/10.1093/bjsw/32.8.997

Bechtel, K. (2010) Sexual abuse and sexually transmitted infections in children and adolescents. *Current Opinion in Pediatrics*, 22(1), 94–9. https://doi.org/10.1097/MOP.0b013e32833502ad

Beeghley, L. (1988) Individual and structural explanations of poverty. *Population Research and Policy Review*, 7(3), 201–22. Available at: www.jstor.org/stable/40229945

Bent-Goodley, T.B. (2014) Social work: a profession of power, passion, and purpose. *Social Work*, 59(3), 197–9. https://doi.org/10.1093/sw/swu019

Bierstedt, R. (1950) An analysis of social power. *American Sociological Review*, 15(6), 730–8.

Blumenthal, S., Gudjonsson, G. and Burns, J. (1999) Cognitive distortions and blame attribution in sex offenders against adults and children. *Child Abuse and Neglect*, 23(2), 129–43. https://doi.org/10.1016/s0145-2134(98)00117-3

Bowlby, J. (1988) *A Secure Base: Parent-Child Attachment and Healthy Human Development*. New York: Basic Books.

Braye, S., Orr, D. and Preston-Shoot, M. (2017) Autonomy and protection in self-neglect work: the ethical complexity of decision-making. *Ethics and Social Welfare*, 11(4), 320–35. https://doi.org/10.1080/17496535.2017.1290814

Brennan, C. (2015) Trials and contestations: Ireland's Ryan Commission. In J. Skold and S. Swain (eds), *Apologies and the Legacy of Abuse of Children in 'Care'*. Basingstoke: Palgrave Macmillan, pp. 55–69.

British Association of Social Workers (BASW) (2021) *Code of Ethics for Social Work*. Available at: https://basw.co.uk/sites/default/files/resources/basw_code_of_ethics_-_2021.pdf

Bronfenbrenner, U. (1979) *The Ecology of Human Development: Experiments by Nature and Design*. Cambridge, MA: Harvard University Press.

Bywaters, P. and Skinner, G. (2022) *The Relationship Between Poverty and Child Abuse and Neglect: New Evidence*. Huddersfield: University of Huddersfield. Available at: RelationshipBetweenPovertyChildAbuseandNeglect_Report.pdf

Care Act 2014. Available at: www.legislation.gov.uk/ukpga/2014/23/contents/enacted

Casey, L. (2025) *National Audit on Group-Based Child Sexual Exploitation and Abuse*. Available at: https://assets.publishing.service.gov.uk/media/685559d05225e4ed0bf3ce54/National_Audit_on_Group-based_Child_Sexual_Exploitation_and_Abuse.pdf

Caslini, M., Bartoli, F., Crocamo, C., Dakanalis, A., Clerici, M. and Carrà, G. (2016) Disentangling the association between child abuse and eating disorders: a systematic review and meta-analysis. *Psychosomatic Medicine*, 78(1), 79–90. https://doi.org/10.1097/PSY.0000000000000233

Cavener, J. and Lonbay, S. (2022) Enhancing 'best practice' in trauma-informed social work education: insights from a study exploring educator and student experiences. *Social Work Education*, 43(2), 317–38. https://doi.org/10.1080/02615479.2022.2091128

Cerebra (2023) *Fabricated or Induced Illness: Final Report*. 1 November. Available at: https://cerebra.org.uk/wp-content/uploads/2023/11/FII-Final-report-2023-Nov-01.pdf

Chapman, A.L., Gratz, K.L. and Brown, M.Z. (2006) Solving the puzzle of deliberate self-harm: the experiential avoidance model. *Behaviour Research and Therapy*, 44(3), 371–94. https://doi.org/10.1016/j.brat.2005.03.005

Chen, Y., Shan, Y., Lin, K., Wei, Y., Kim, H., Koenen, K.C., Gelaye, B. and Papatheodorou, S. (2023) Association between child abuse and risk of adult coronary heart disease: a systematic review and meta-analysis. *American Journal of Preventive Medicine*, 65(1), 143–54. https://doi.org/10.1016/j.amepre.2023.02.028

Child Welfare Information Gateway (2023) *Separating Poverty from Neglect in Child Welfare*. Available at: www.childwelfare.gov/topics/prevention/separating-poverty-neglect/?top=89

Children (Equal Protection from Assault) (Scotland) Act 2019. Available at: www.legislation.gov.uk/asp/2019/16

Children Act 1908. Available at: www.legislation.gov.uk/ukpga/1908/67/pdfs/ukpga_19080067_en.pdf

Children Act 1948. Available at: www.education-uk.org/documents/acts/1948-children-act.html

Children Act 1989. Available at: www.legislation.gov.uk/ukpga/1989/41/contents

Children and Families Act 2014. Available at: www.legislation.gov.uk/ukpga/2014/6/contents

Children and Social Work Act 2017. Available at: www.legislation.gov.uk/ukpga/2017/16/contents

Children and Young Persons Act 1933. Available at: www.legislation.gov.uk/ukpga/Geo5/23-24/12

Children and Young Persons Act 1963. Available at: www.legislation.gov.uk/ukpga/1963/37/contents/enacted

Children (Northern Ireland) Order 1995. Available at: www.legislation.gov.uk/nisi/1995/755/contents/made

Children (Scotland) Act 1995. Available at: www.legislation.gov.uk/ukpga/1995/36/contents

Christoffersen, A. (2021) *Intersectionality in Practice: A Guide for Social Workers and Other Professionals*. Edinburgh: University of Edinburgh. Available at: www.intersectionalityinpractice.ed.ac.uk/wp-content/uploads/2021/09/Intersectionality-in-practice.pdf

Cockbain, E. and Tufail, W. (2020) Failing victims, fuelling hate: challenging the harms of the 'Muslim grooming gangs' narrative. *Race and Class*, 61(2), 21–36. https://doi.org/10.1177/0306396819895727

Cocker, C. and Hafford-Letchfield, T. (eds) (2014) *Rethinking Anti-discriminatory and Anti-oppressive Theories for Social Work Practice*. Basingstoke: Palgrave Macmillan.

Colman, R.A. and Widom, C.S. (2004) Childhood abuse and neglect and adult intimate relationships: a prospective study. *Child Abuse and Neglect*, 28(11), 1133–51. ISSN 0145-2134, https://doi.org/10.1016/j.chiabu.2004.02.005

Conger, K.J., Ructer, M.A. and Conger, R.D. (2000) The role of economic pressure in the lives of parents and their adolescents: the family stress model. In L.J. Crockett and R.K. Silbereisen (eds), *Negotiating Adolescence in Times of Change*. Cambridge: Cambridge University Press, pp. 201–23.

Conrad-Hiebner, A. and Byram, E. (2020) The temporal impact of economic insecurity on child maltreatment: a systematic review. *Trauma, Violence and Abuse*, 21(1), 157–78. https://doi.org/10.1177/1524838018756122

Conti, G., Pizzo, E., Morris, S. and Melnychuk, M. (2021) The economic costs of child maltreatment in the UK. *Health Economics*, 31(2), 340–59. https://doi.org/10.1002/hec.4409

Corby, B., Doig, A. and Roberts, V. (1998) Inquiries into child abuse. *Journal of Social Welfare and Family Law*, 20(4), 377–95.

Corby, B., Shemmings, D. and Wilkins, D. (2012) *Child Abuse: An Evidence Base for Confident Practice*. 4th edn. Maidenhead: Open University Press.

Corrigan, P. and Leonard, P. (1978) *Social Work Practice under Capitalism*. Basingstoke: Macmillan.

Cowden, S. and Singh, G. (2013) *Is Cultural Sensitivity Always a Good Thing? Arguments for a Universalist Social Work. In: Practical Social Work Ethics*. Abingdon: Ashgate, pp. 63–82. ISBN 9781409438250

CPS (2024) *Man Who Used AI Technology to Create Child Sexual Abuse Images Jailed*. Available at: www.cps.gov.uk/cps/news/man-who-used-ai-technology-create-child-sexual-abuse-images-jailed

Crawford, M. (2020) Ecological systems theory: exploring the development of the theoretical framework as conceived by Bronfenbrenner. *Journal of Public Health Issues and Practice*, 4(2), 170.

Crenshaw, K. (1989) Demarginalizing the intersection of race and sex: a Black feminist critique of antidiscrimination doctrine, feminist theory and antiracist politics. *University of Chicago Legal Forum*, 1989(1), 139–67.

Crenshaw, K. (1991) Mapping the margins: intersectionality, identity politics, and violence against women of color. *Stanford Law Review*, 43(6), 1241–99.

Crime Survey for England and Wales (CSEW) (various years). Available at: www.crimesurvey.co.uk/en/index.html

Criminal Injuries Compensation Authority (CICA) (n.d.) *Historical Abuse Compensation*. Available at: www.cica-uk.co.uk/historical-abuse-compensation/#:~:text=Sometimes%20called%20non%2Drecent%20abuse,of%20what%20they%20went%20through.

Crozier, J.C. and Barth, R.P. (2005) Cognitive and academic functioning in maltreated children. *Children and Schools*, 27(4), 197–206. https://doi.org/10.1093/cs/27.4.197

CSA Centre (2023) *Signs and Indicators of Child Sexual Abuse*. Available at: www.csacentre.org.uk/app/uploads/2023/09/Signs-and-Indicators-Template.pdf

Currie, J. and Widom, C.S. (2010) Long-term consequences of child abuse and neglect on adult economic well-being. *Child Maltreatment*, 15(2), 111–20. https://doi.org/10.1177/1077559509355316

Dahl, R.A. (1957) The concept of power. *Behavioral Science*, 2(3), 201–15.

Dalrymple, J. and Burke, B. (2006) *Anti-oppressive Practice: Social Care and the* Law. 2nd edn. Maidenhead: Open University Press.

Danese, A. and McEwen, B S. (2012) Adverse childhood experiences, allostasis, allostatic load, and age-related disease. *Physiology and Behavior*, 106(1), 29–39. https://doi.org/10.1016/j.physbeh.2011.08.019

Daniels, J.K., Timmerman, M.E., Spitzer, C. and Lampe, A. (2024) Differential constellations of dissociative symptoms and their association with childhood trauma: a latent profile analysis. *European Journal of Psychotraumatology*, 15(1). https://doi.org/10.1080/20008066.2024.2348345

Darling, A.J. (2018) Understanding female-perpetrated child sexual abuse in organisational contexts. Doctoral thesis, Durham University. Durham E-Theses Online. Available at: http://etheses.dur.ac.uk/12768/

Data Protection Act (DPA) 2018. Available at: www.legislation.gov.uk/ukpga/2018/12/contents

Dawes, A., Kropiwnicki, Z.D.S., Kafaar, Z. and Richter, L. (2005) *Corporal Punishment of Children: A South African National Survey*. Cape Town: HSRC.

Delap, L. (2015) Child welfare, child protection and sexual abuse, 1918–1990. *History and Policy*. Available at: www.historyandpolicy.org/policy-papers/papers/child-welfare-child-protection-and-sexual-abuse-1918-1990

Department for Children, Schools and Families (DCSF) (2009) *Safeguarding Children and Young People from Sexual Exploitation*. Available at: https://dera.ioe.ac.uk/id/eprint/9329/1/00689-2009BKT-EN.pdf

Department for Education (DfE) (2014) *Delegation of Authority to Carers: Young People's Guide*. Available at: https://assets.publishing.service.gov.uk/government/uploads/system/uploads/attachment_data/file/305147/Delegation_of_authority_to_carers_YP_version.pdf

DfE (2017) *Child Sexual Exploitation: Definition and a Guide for Practitioners, Local Leaders and Decision Makers Working to Protect Children from Child Sexual Exploitation*. Available at: https://assets.publishing.service.gov.uk/government/uploads/system/uploads/attachment_data/file/591903/CSE_Guidance_Core_Document_13.02.2017.pdf

DfE (2021a) *Safeguarding and Radicalisation: Learning from Children's Social Care*. Available at: www.gov.uk/government/publications/safeguarding-and-radicalisation-childrens-social-care-learning

DfE (2021b) *The Children Act 1989: Guidance and Regulations. Volume 2 – Care Planning, Placement and Case Review*. Available at: https://assets.publishing.service.gov.uk/government/uploads/system/uploads/attachment_data/file/1000549/The_Children_Act_1989_guidance_and_regulations_Volume_2_care_planning__p

DfE (2023) *Working Together to Safeguard Children*. Available at: www.gov.uk/government/publications/working-together-to-safeguard-children--2

Department for Education and Skills (DfES) (2003) *Every Child Matters*. London: HMSO. A>4998-DfES-ChildrenGPaperCOV

Department for Levelling Up, Housing and Communities (DLUHC) (2022) *Early Help System Guide*. Available at: https://assets.publishing.service.gov.uk/media/628de13be90e071f5f7e1bd2/Early_Help_System_Guide.p

Department for Science, Innovation and Technology (DSIT) (2023) *Online Safety Act Explainer*. Available at: www.gov.uk/government/publications/online-safety-act-explainer/online-safety-act-explainer

Department of Health (DoH) (1995) *Child Protection: Messages from Research*. London: HMSO.

DoH (2000) *Lost in Care Report of the Tribunal of Inquiry into the Abuse of Children in Care in the Former County Council Areas of Gwynedd and Clwyd since 1974*. Available at: https://webarchive.nationalarchives.gov.uk/ukgwa/20130123203807/http://www.dh.gov.uk/en/Publicationsandstatistics/Publications/PublicationsPolicyAndGuidance/DH_4003097

DoH (2015) *Knowledge and Skills Statement for Social Workers in Adult Services*. Available at: https://assets.publishing.service.gov.uk/media/5a808324ed915d74e622ee26/KSS.pdf

DoH, Department for Education and Employment (DfEE) and the Home Office (HO) (2000) *Framework for the Assessment of Children in Need and their Families*. London: HMSO.

Department of Health and Social Care (DoHSC) (2019) *Strengths-Based Approach Practice Framework and Handbook*. Available at: https://assets.publishing.service.gov.uk/media/5c62ae87ed915d04446a5739/stengths-based-approach-practice-framework-and-handbook.pdf

DoHSC (2023) *Care and Support Statutory Guidance*. Available at: www.gov.uk/government/publications/care-act-statutory-guidance/care-and-support-statutory-guidance

Department of Health, Social Services and Public Safety/Department of Justice (DHSSPS/DoJ) (2015) *Adult Safeguarding: Prevention and Protection in Partnership*. Available at: www.rqia.org.uk/RQIA/files/ad/addb8d4d-7a71-4393-be47-1b4a1b3696b1.pdf

Department of Health Northern Ireland (DoH-NI) (2017) *Co-operating to Safeguard Children and Young People in Northern Ireland*. Available at: www.health-ni.gov.uk/publications/co-operating-safeguard-children-and-young-people-northern-ireland

Devlieghere, J. and Gillingham, P. (2021) Transparency in social work: a critical exploration and reflection. *British Journal of Social Work*, 51(8), 3375–92. https://doi.org/10.1093/bjsw/bcaa166

Devries, K., Knight, L., Petzold, M. … and Abrahams, N. (2018) Who perpetrates violence against children? A systematic analysis of age-specific and sex-specific data. *BMJ Paediatrics Open*. https://doi.org/10.1136/bmjpo-2017-000180

Dillon, J. (2021) 'Wishes and feelings': misunderstandings and missed opportunities for participation in child protection proceedings. *Child and Family Social Work*, 26(4), 664–76. https://doi.org/10.1111/cfs.12847

Dixon, L., Browne, K. and Hamilton-Giachritsis, C. (2008) Patterns of risk and protective factors in the intergenerational cycle of maltreatment. *Journal of Family Violence*, 24, 111–22 (2009). https://doi.org/10.1007/s10896-008-9215-2

Dixon, L., Hamilton-Giachritsis, C. and Browne, K. (2005) Attributions and behaviours of parents abused as children: a mediational analysis of the intergenerational continuity of child maltreatment (Part II). *Journal of Child Psychology and Psychiatry*, 46(1), 58–68. https://doi.org/10.1111/j.1469-7610.2004.00340.x

Dominelli, L. (2002a) *Feminist Social Work Theory and Practice*. Basingstoke: Palgrave Macmillan.

Dominelli, L. (2002b) *Anti-oppressive Social Work Theory and Practice*. Basingstoke: Palgrave Macmillan.

Dons, G., Naert, J. and Roose, R. (2022) Transparency in social work: mapping polarities faced by social workers. *British Journal of Social Work*, 52(8), 5066–83. https://doi.org/10.1093/bjsw/bcac095

Dube, S.R., Fairweather, D., Pearson, W.S., Felitti, V.J., Anda, R.F. and Croft, J.B. (2009) Cumulative childhood stress and autoimmune diseases in adults. *Psychosomatic Medicine*, 71(2), 243–50. https://doi.org/10.1097/PSY.0b013e3181907888

Durrant, J. and Ensom, R. (2012) Physical punishment of children: lessons from 20 years of research. *Canadian Medical Association Journal (Journal de l'Association medicale canadienne)*, 184(12), 1373–7. https://doi.org/10.1503/cmaj.101314

Eckenrode, J., Smith, E.G., McCarthy, M.E. and Dineen, M. (2014) Income inequality and child maltreatment in the United States. *Pediatrics*, 133(3), 454–61. https://doi.org/10.1542/peds.2013-1707

Elliott, G., Cunningham, S., Linder, M., Colangelo, M. and Lilly, M. (2005) Child physical abuse and self-perceived social isolation among adolescents. *Journal of Interpersonal Violence*, 20, 1663–84. 10.1177/0886260505281439

Elsley, S. (2017) *Review of Societal Attitudes of Children for the Scottish Child Abuse Inquiry*. Available at: societal-attitudes-review-susan-elsley-may-2017.pdf

Female Genital Mutilation Act 2003. Available at: www.legislation.gov.uk/ukpga/2003/31/pdfs/ukpga_20030031_en.pdf

Ferguson, H. (2007) Abused and looked after children as 'moral dirt': child abuse and institutional care in historical perspective. *Journal of Social Policy*, 36(1), 123–39. doi:10.1017/S0047279406000407

Ferguson, H., Warwick, L., Disney, T., Leigh, J. and Cooner, T.S. (2020) The nature and culture of social work with children and families in long-term casework: findings from a qualitative longitudinal study. *Social Work Education*, 40(2), 204–22. https://doi.org/10.1080/02615479.2020.1837105

Finkelhor, D. (1984) *Child Sexual Abuse: New Theory and Research*. New York: Free Press.

Finkelhor, D., Ormrod, R.K. and Turner, H.A. (2007) Poly-victimization: a neglected component in child victimization. *Child Abuse and Neglect*, 33(7), 287–90.

Fisher-Borne, M., Cain, J.M. and Martin, S.L. (2014) From mastery to accountability: cultural humility as an alternative to cultural competence. *Social Work Education*, 34(2), 165–81. https://doi.org/10.1080/02615479.2014.977244

Fleming, J., Mullen, P.E., Sibthorpe, B. and Bammer, G. (1999) The long-term impact of childhood sexual abuse in Australian women. *Child Abuse and Neglect*, 23(2), 145-59.

Fontes, L.A. (2005) *Child Abuse and Culture: Working with Diverse Families*. London: Guilford Press.

Fook, J. (2012) *Social Work: A Critical Practice Approach* (2nd edn). London: Sage.

Foucault, M. (1982) The subject and power. *Critical Inquiry*, 8(4), 777–95.

Frizell, E. (2009) *Independent Inquiry into Abuse at Kerelew Residential School and Secure Unit*. Edinburgh: Scottish Government.

Fucà, E., Guerrera, S., Falvo, S., Sestito, S., De Rose, P. and Vicari, S. (2024) Characterization of sleep difficulties in maltreated children and adolescents. *European Journal of Pediatrics*, 183(10), 4445–55. https://doi.org/10.1007/s00431-024-05718-w

Galinsky, A.D., Gruenfeld, D.H. and Magee, J.C. (2003) From power to action. *Journal of Personality and Social Psychology*, 85, 453–66. 10.1037/0022-3514.85.3.453

Garofalo, C. and Bogaerts, S. (2019) Attachment and personality disorders among child molesters: the role of trust. *Sexual Abuse: A Journal of Research and Treatment*, 31(1), 97–124. https://doi.org/10.1177/1079063217720928

Gaventa, J. (2003) *Power after Lukes: A Review of the Literature*. Brighton: Institute of Development Studies.

Gawne, E. (2024, October 28) Man who made 'depraved' child images with AI jailed. *BBC News*. Available at: www.bbc.co.uk/news/articles/cq6l241z5mjo

Gelles, R.J. (1992) Poverty and violence toward children. *American Behavioral Scientist*, 35(3), 258–74. https://doi.org/10.1177/0002764292035003005

Germain, C.B. and Gitterman, A. (1980) *The Life Model of Social Work Practice*. New York: Columbia University Press.

Gershoff, E.T. (2002) Corporal punishment by parents and associated child behaviors and experiences: a meta-analytic and theoretical review. *Psychological Bulletin*, 128(4), 539–79. https://doi.org/10.1037/0033-2909.128.4.539

Gibbs, J., Coughlan, B., Morgan, T., Mikushnica, A., Phippard, S., Crozier-Roche, F., Drayak, T., Graham, D., Smith, J. and Duschinsky, R. (2024) Social workers' perceptions of the nature of child neglect: a systematic literature review. *British Journal of Social Work*, 54(8), 3619–37. https://doi.org/10.1093/bjsw/bcae102

Giddens, A. (1984) *The Constitution of Society: Outline of the Theory of Structuration*. Los Angeles: University of California Press.

Gil, D.G. (1975) Unraveling child abuse. *American Journal of Orthopsychiatry*, 45(3), 346–56. https://doi.org/10.1111/j.1939-0025.1975.tb02545.x

Gillick v West Norfolk and Wisbech AHA [1985] *UKHL 7*.

Glaser, D. (2002) Emotional abuse and neglect (psychological maltreatment): a conceptual framework. *Child Abuse and Neglect*, 26(6–7), 697–714. https://doi.org/10.1016/S0145-2134(02)00342-3

Glasser, M., Kolvin, I., Campbell, D., Glasser, A., Leitch, I. and Farrelly S. (2001) Cycle of child sexual abuse: links between being a victim and becoming a perpetrator. *British Journal of Psychiatry*, 179(6), 482–94. doi:10.1192/bjp.179.6.482

Goddard, A. (2021) Adverse childhood experiences and trauma-informed care. *Journal of Pediatric Health Care*, 35(2), 145–55. https://doi.org/10.1016/j.pedhc.2020.09.001

Gottlieb, M. (2020) The case for a cultural humility framework in social work practice. *Journal of Ethnic and Cultural Diversity in Social Work*, 30(6), 463–81. https://doi.org/10.1080/15313204.2020.1753615

Gratz, K.L. (2001) Measurement of deliberate self-harm: preliminary data on the deliberate self-harm inventory. *Journal of Psychopathology and Behavioral Assessment*, 23(4), 253–63. https://doi.org/10.1023/A:1012779403943

Greene, C.A., Haisley, L., Wallace, C. and Ford, J.D. (2020) Intergenerational effects of childhood maltreatment: a systematic review of the parenting practices of adult survivors of childhood abuse, neglect, and violence. *Clinical Psychology Review*, 80, 101891. https://doi.org/10.1016/j.cpr.2020.101891

Harper, K. (2006) Negotiating therapeutic boundaries with childhood sexual abuse survivors: choices in decision-making. *Stress, Trauma and Crisis: An International Journal*, 9, 95–117.

Hart, A. (Chair) (2017) *Report of the Historical Institutional Abuse Inquiry*. The Executive Office, Northern Ireland.

Haugaard, M. (2010) Power: a 'family resemblance' concept. *European Journal of Cultural Studies*, 13(4), 419–38. 10.1177/1367549410377152

Haworth, S., Schaub, J., Kidney, E. and Montgomery, P. (2024) A systematic review of measures of child neglect. *Research on Social Work Practice*, 34(1), 17–40. https://doi.org/10.1177/10497315221138066

Hawthorn, M. (2006) Historic abuse in residential care: sharing good practice. *In Residence No 4*. Glasgow: Scottish Institute for Residential Child Care.

Health and Care Professions Council (HCPC) (2025) *HCPC Corporate Plan 2025–26*. Available at: www.hcpc-uk.org/globalassets/resources/2025/hcpc-corporate-plan-2025-26.pdf?v=638804130060000000

Home Office (HO) (2020a) *Group-Based Child Sexual Exploitation: Characteristics of Offending*. Available at: www.gov.uk/government/publications/group-based-child-sexual-exploitation-characteristics-of-offending

HO (2020b) *Multi-Agency Statutory Guidance on Female Genital Mutilation*. Available at: https://assets.publishing.service.gov.uk/media/613f26d5e90e07044435c949/6.7166_HO_FBIS_BN_O__Leaflet_A4_FINAL_080321_WEB.pdf

HO (2021) *The Economic and Social Cost of Contact Child Sexual Abuse*. Available at: www.gov.uk/government/publications/the-economic-and-social-cost-of-contact-child-sexual-abuse

Hoque, M.M. (2021) Reviewing child labour and its worst forms: contemporary theoretical and policy agenda. *Journal of Modern Slavery*, 6(4). 10.22150/jms/PAZE6574.

Horwitz, A.V., Widom, C.S., McLaughlin, J. and White, H.R. (2001) The impact of childhood abuse and neglect on adult mental health: a prospective study. *Journal of Health and Social Behavior*, 42(2), 184–201.

House of Lords Public Services Committee (2021) Children in Crisis: The Role of Public Services in Overcoming Child Vulnerability. *House of Lords Library*. Available at: https://lordslibrary.parliament.uk/public-services-committee-report-role-of-public-services-in-supporting-vulnerable-children/

Independent Inquiry into Child Sexual Abuse (IICSA) (2018) *Effects of Child Sexual Abuse*. Available at: www.iicsa.org.uk/reports-recommendations/publications/inquiry/interim/nature-effects-child-sexual-abuse/effects-child-sexual-abuse.html

IICSA (2022a) *Child Sexual Exploitation by Organised Networks Investigation Report*. Available at: www.iicsa.org.uk/reports-recommendations/publications/investigation/cs-organised-networks

IICSA (2022b) *The Report of the Independent Inquiry into Child Sexual Abuse*. Available at: https://assets.publishing.service.gov.uk/media/634febd6d3bf7f618eda953d/the-report-independent-inquiry-into-child-sexual-abuse-october-2022.pdf

Inesi, M.E., Botti, S., Dubois, D., Rucker, D.D. and Galinsky, A.D. (2011) Power and choice: their dynamic interplay in quenching the thirst for personal control. *Psychological Science*, 22(8), 1042–8. https://doi.org/10.1177/0956797611413936 (original work published 2011).

Information Commissioner's Office (ICO) (n.d.) *A 10 Step Guide to Sharing Information to Safeguard Children*. Available at: https://ico.org.uk/for-organisations/uk-gdpr-guidance-and-resources/data-sharing/a-10-step-guide-to-sharing-information-to-safeguard-children/

Infurna, M.R., Reichl, C., Parzer, P., Schimmenti, A., Bifulco, A. and Kaess, M. (2016) Associations between depression and specific childhood experiences of abuse and neglect: a meta-analysis. *Journal of Affective Disorders*, 190, 47–55. https://doi.org/10.1016/j.jad.2015.09.006

Ingram, R. and Smith, M. (2018) Relationship-based practice: emergent themes in social work literature. *IRISS Insight*, 41. Available at: www.iriss.org.uk/resources/insights/relationship-based-practice-emergent-themes-social-work-literature

International Labour Organization (ILO) (1999) *Worst Forms of Child Labour Convention*. Available at: https://normlex.ilo.org/dyn/nrmlx_en/f?p=NORMLEXPUB:12100:0::NO::P12100_ILO_CODE:C182

ILO (2020) *Child Labour: Global Estimates 2020, Trends and the Road Forward*. Available at: www.ilo.org/publications/major-publications/child-labour-global-estimates-2020-trends-and-road-forward

Internet Watch Foundation (IWF) (2025) *Child Sexual Abuse Material vs 'Child Porn': Why Language Matters*. Available at: www.iwf.org.uk/news-media/blogs/child-sexual-abuse-material-vs-child-porn-why-language-matters/

Jenkinson, A. and Chamberlain, J. (2019) How misinterpretation of 'unwise decisions' principle illustrates value of legal literacy for social workers. *Community Care*. Available at: www.communitycare.co.uk/2019/06/28/misinterpretation-unwise-decisions-principle-illustrates-value-legal-literacy-social-workers/

Jenks, C. (2005) *Childhood*. 2nd edn. London: Routledge.

Jespersen, A.F., Lalumière, M.L. and Seto, M.C. (2009) Sexual abuse history among adult sex offenders and non-sex offenders: a meta-analysis. *Child Abuse and Neglect*, 33(3), 179–92. https://doi.org/10.1016/j.chiabu.2008.07.004

Johnson, K. and Boland, B. (2019) Adult safeguarding under the Care Act 2014. *British Journal of Psychology bulletin*, 43(1), 38–42. https://doi.org/10.1192/bjb.2018.71

Jones, K. (2021) Fabricated or induced illness. *Safeguarding Network*. Available at: https://safeguarding.network/content-delivery/fabricated-or-induced-illness/

Karim, S. (2017) Why 'historic' abuse? Experiences of children reporting abuse historically. *Scottish Journal of Residential Child Care*, 16(3), 1–12.

Karim, S. (2020) Power and the historic abuse of children in care. Doctoral thesis, University of Strathclyde, Glasgow.

Karim, S. (2023) Power-informed practice in social work. *Journal of Social Work*, 23(6), 1062–79. https://doi.org/10.1177/14680173231180307 (original work published 2023).

Karlsen, S., Howard, J., Carver, N., Mogilnicka, M. and Pantazis, C. (2023) Available evidence suggests that prevalence and risk of female genital cutting/mutilation in the UK is much lower than widely presumed: policies based on exaggerated estimates are harmful to girls and women from affected communities. *International Journal of Impotence Research*, 35(3), 212–15. https://doi.org/10.1038/s41443-021-00526-4

Karsna, K. and Kelly, L. (2021) The Scale and Nature of Child Sexual Abuse: Review of Evidence. *Centre of Expertise on Child Sexual Abuse*. Available at: www.csacentre.org.uk/app/uploads/2023/09/Scale-and-nature-review-of-evidence-2021.pdf

Kavenagh, M. (2022) *Child Sexual Exploitation in Online Gaming: Risks and Realities*. UNICEF. Available at: www.unicef.org/eap/blog/child-sexual-exploitation-online-gaming

Keddell, E. (2016) Interpreting children's best interests: needs, attachment and decision-making. *Journal of Social Work*, 17(3), 324–42. https://doi.org/10.1177/1468017316644694

Kent, A., Waller, G. and Dagnan, D. (1999) A greater role of emotional than physical or sexual abuse in predicting disordered eating attitudes: the role of mediating variables. *International Journal of Eating Disorders*,25(2),159–67.https://doi.org/10.1002/(sici)1098-108x(199903)25:2<159::aid-eat5>3.0.co;2-f

Kilkelly, U. (2020) Health rights of children. In J. Todres and S.M. King (eds), *The Oxford Handbook of Children's Rights*. Oxford: Oxford University Press.

Kim, H. and Drake, B. (2023) Has the relationship between community poverty and child maltreatment report rates become stronger or weaker over time? *Child Abuse and Neglect*, 143, 106333. https://doi.org/10.1016/j.chiabu.2023.106333

Kirkwood, A. (1993) *The Leicestershire Inquiry, 1992: The Report of an Inquiry into Aspects of the Management of Children's Homes in Leicestershire between 1973 and 1986*. Leicester: Leicestershire County Council.

Kitzinger, J. (2004) *Framing Abuse: Media Influence and Public Understanding of Sexual Violence against Children*. London: Pluto.

Klonsky, E.D. and May, A.M. (2015) The Three-Step Theory (3ST): a new theory of suicide rooted in the 'ideation-to-action' framework. *International Journal of Cognitive Therapy*, 8(2), 114–28. https://doi.org/10.1521/ijct.2015.8.2.114

Knight, C. (2015) Trauma-informed social work practice: practice considerations and challenges. *Clinical Social Work Journal*, 43(1), 25–37. https://doi.org/10.1007/s10615-014-0481-6

Knight, C. (2019) Trauma informed practice and care: implications for field instruction. *Clinical Social Work Journal*, 47, 79–89. https://doi.org/10.1007/s10615-018-0661-x

Korbin, J.E. (2002) Culture and child maltreatment: cultural competence and beyond. *Child Abuse and Neglect*, 26(6–7), 637–44.

Laajasalo, T., Cowley, L.E., Otterman, G., Lamela, D., Rodrigues, L.B., Jud, A., Kemp, A., Naughton, A., Hurt, L., Soldino, V., Ntinapogias, A., Nurmatov, U. and COST Action Network 19106 (2023) Current issues and challenges in the definition and operationalization of child maltreatment: a scoping review. *Child Abuse and Neglect*, 140. 106187. 10.1016/j.chiabu.2023.106187

Laird, S.E. and Tedam, P. (2019) *Cultural Diversity in Child Protection: Cultural Competence in Practice*. London: Red Globe Press and Macmillan International.

Laming (2003) *The Victoria Climbié Inquiry: Report of an Inquiry by Lord Laming*. Available at: https://assets.publishing.service.gov.uk/media/5a7c5edeed915d696ccfc51b/5730.pdf

Lammers, J., Stoker, J.I., Rink, F. and Galinsky, A.D. (2016) To have control over or to be free from others? The desire for power reflects a need for autonomy. *Personality and Social Psychology Bulletin*, 42(4), 498–512. https://doi.org/10.1177/0146167216634064

League of Nations (1924) *Geneva Declaration of the Rights of the Child*. Available at: www.un-documents.net/gdrc1924.htm#:~:text=By%20the%20present%20Declaration%20of,from%20United%20Nations%20web%20sites

Leclerc, B. and Proulx, J. (2018) An opportunity view of child sexual offending: investigating nonpersuasion and circumstances of offending through criminological lens. *Sexual Abuse: A Journal of Research and Treatment*, 30(7), 869–82. https://doi.org/10.1177/1079063217729158

Leonardsen, M. (2007) Empowerment in social work: an individual vs a relational perspective. *International Journal of Social Welfare*, 16, 3–11. https://doi.org/10.1111/j.1468-2397.2006.00449.x

Levenson, J. (2017) Trauma-informed social work practice. *Social Work*, 62(2), 105–13. https://doi.org/10.1093/sw/swx001

Levin, I., Haldar, M. and Picot, A. (2015) Social work and sociology: historical separation and current challenges. *Nordic Social Work Research*, 5(sup1), 1–6. doi: 10.1080/2156857X.2015.1068503

Li, M., D'Arcy, C. and Meng, X. (2016) Maltreatment in childhood substantially increases the risk of adult depression and anxiety in prospective cohort studies: systematic review, meta-analysis, and proportional attributable fractions. *Psychological Medicine*, 46(4), 717–30. doi:10.1017/S0033291715002743

Lindsay, T., Parker, J., Lindsay, T. and Bradley, G. (2013) *Person-centred Approaches*. 2nd edn. London: Sage, pp. 19–34. https://doi.org/10.4135/9781526435712

Livingstone S., Davidson J., Bryce J., Batool S., Haughton C. and Nandi A. (2017) *Children's Online Activities, Risks and Safety: A Literature Review by the UKCCIS Evidence Group*. Available at: www.gov.uk/government/uploads/system/uploads/attachment_data/file/650933/Literature_Review_Final_October_2017.pdf

Lonne, B., Harries, M., Featherstone, B. and Gray, M. (2016) *Working Ethically in Child Protection*. London: Routledge. https://doi.org/10.4324/9781315851020

Lukes, S. (1986) *Power*. New York: New York University Press.

MacAlister, J. (2022) *The Independent Review of Children's Social Care: Final Report*. DfE. https://assets.publishing.service.gov.uk/media/640a17f28fa8f5560820da4b/Independent_review_of_children_s_social_care_-_Final_report.pdf

Macpherson, J.M., Gray, S.R., Ip, P., McCallum, M., Hanlon, P., Welsh, P., Chan, K.L., Mair, F.S., Celis-Morales, C., Minnis, H., Pell, J.P. and Ho, F.K. (2021) Child maltreatment and incident mental disorders in middle and older ages: a retrospective UK Biobank cohort study. *The Lancet Regional Health: Europe*, 11, 100224. https://doi.org/10.1016/j.lanepe.2021.100224

Madigan, S., Cyr, C., Eirich, R., Fearon, R.M.P., Ly, A., Rash, C., Poole, J.C. and Alink, L.R.A. (2019) Testing the cycle of maltreatment hypothesis: meta-analytic evidence of the intergenerational transmission of child maltreatment. *Development and Psychopathology*, 31(1), 23–51. https://doi.org/10.1017/S0954579418001700

Manly, J.T., Cicchetti, D. and Barnett, D. (1994) The impact of subtype, frequency, chronicity, and severity of child maltreatment on social competence and behavior problems. *Development and Psychopathology*, 6(1), 121–43. doi:10.1017/S0954579400005915

Manus, S., Lubian, K., Bennett, C., Turley, C., Porter, L., Gill, V., with Gunnell, D. and Weich, S. (2019) *Suicide and Selfharm in Britain: Researching Risk and Resilience using UK Surveys - Summary*. NatCen: London.

Marshall, K., Jamieson, C. and Finlayson, A. (1999) *Edinburgh's Children: The Edinburgh Inquiry into the Abuse and Protection of Children in Care*. Edinburgh: Edinburgh City Council.

Martin, P. and Mbambo, B. (2011) An Exploratory Study on the Interplay between African Customary Law and Practices and Children's Protection Rights in South Africa. *Save the Children*. Available at: www.childlinesa.org.za/wp-content/uploads/customary-law-study-south-africa-report-nov-2011.pdf

Mathews, B. and Collin-Vézina, D. (2019) Child sexual abuse: toward a conceptual model and definition. *Trauma, Violence and Abuse*, 20(2), 131–48. https://doi.org/10.1177/1524838017738726

Maxwell, J. (2016) 'Two systems of law side by side': the role of indigenous customary law in sentencing. *Australian Indigenous Law Review*, 97. Available at: https://ssrn.com/abstract=3885309 or http://dx.doi.org/10.2139/ssrn.3885309

McLaughlin, K. (2016) *Empowerment: A Critique*. London: Routledge. https://doi.org/10.4324/9781315744339

Mental Capacity Act (Northern Ireland) 2016. Available at: www.legislation.gov.uk/nia/2016/18/contents/enacted

Mental Capacity Act 2005. Available at: www.legislation.gov.uk/ukpga/2005/9/contents

Millstein, K. (2000) Confidentiality in direct social-work practice: inevitable challenges and ethical dilemmas. *Families in Society*, 81(3), 270–82. https://doi.org/10.1606/1044-3894.1018

Ministry of Justice (2023) The Public Law Outline (PLO) – Revised Version. *HM Courts and Tribunals Service*. Available at: www.justice.gov.uk/courts/procedure-rules/family/practice_directions/pd_part_12a

Mitra, P. and Jain, A. (2023) Dissociative identity disorder. *StatPearls*. Treasure Island, FL: StatPearls. Available at: www.ncbi.nlm.nih.gov/books/NBK568768/

Morris, K. (2013) Troubled families: vulnerable families' experiences of multiple service use. *Child and Family Social Work*, 18. 10.1111/j.1365-2206.2011.00822.x

Morriss, P. (2002) *Power: A Philosophical Analysis*. 2nd edn. Manchester: University of Manchester Press.

Munir, S.A. and Umer, R. (2023) Exploring the causes of child labour and its adverse implications on children's education. *Global Anthropological Studies Review*, 6(1), 32–41. https://doi.org/10.31703/gasr.2023(VI-I)04

Murphy, D., Duggan, M. and Joseph, S. (2013) Relationship-based social work and its compatibility with the person-centred approach: principled versus instrumental perspectives. *British Journal of Social Work*, 43(4), 703–19, https://doi.org/10.1093/bjsw/bcs003

Muzaffar, M. (2025) Musk's X 'amplified Islamophobia, hate speech and disinformation' in grooming gangs debate, damning report says. *The Independent*. Available at: www.independent.co.uk/news/uk/home-news/elon-musk-islamophobia-grooming-gangs-report-b2747829.html

Nadan, Y. and Korbin, J. (2018) Cultural context, intersectionality, and child vulnerability. *Childhood Vulnerability*, 1, 5–14. https://doi.org/10.1007/s41255-019-00003-7

Nardello, R. (2017) Child abuse in a medical setting: case illustrations of two variants of munchausen syndrome by proxy. *EuroMediterranean Biomedical Journal*, 12(10), 047–050. doi:10.3269/1970-5492.2017.12.10

National Association of Social Workers (NASW) (2015) *Standards and Indicators for Cultural Competence in Social Work Practice*. Available at: www.socialworkers.org/Practice/NASW-Practice-Standards-Guidelines/Standards-and-Indicators-for-Cultural-Competence-in-Social-Work-Practice

National Institute for Health and Care Excellence (NICE) (2017) *When to Suspect Child Maltreatment: Neglect: Failure of Provision and Failure of Supervision (NICE Guideline CG89)*. Available at: www.nice.org.uk/guidance/cg89/chapter/Recommendations#neglect-failure-of-provision-and-failure-of-supervision

National Police Chiefs' Council (NPCC) (2024) *Child Sexual Abuse and Exploitation Analysis Launched* [press release]. Vulnerability Knowledge and Practice Programme. Available at: https://news.npcc.police.uk/releases/vkpp-launch-national-analysis-of-police-recorded-child-sexual-abuse-and-exploitation-csae-crimes-report-2022#:~:text=harm%20cases%20with%20high%20community,indecent%20images%20and%20younger%20children

National Research Council (NRC) (2014) *New Directions in Child Abuse and Neglect Research*. Washington, DC: National Academies Press. https://doi.org/10.17226/18331

National Society for the Prevention of Cruelty to Children (NSPCC) (2014) *Culture and Faith: Learning from Case Reviews*. NSPCC Learning. Available at: https://learning.nspcc.org.uk/media/1332/learning-from-case-reviews_culture-and-faith.pdf

NSPCC (2023) *Early Help and Early Intervention*. NSPCC Learning. Available at: https://learning.nspcc.org.uk/safeguarding-child-protection/early-help-and-early-intervention

NSPCC (2024a) *Non-recent Abuse*. Available at: www.nspcc.org.uk/what-is-child-abuse/types-of-abuse/non-recent-abuse/

NSPCC (2024b) *Spotting the Signs of Child Abuse*. Available at: www.nspcc.org.uk/what-is-child-abuse/spotting-signs-child-abuse/

NSPCC (2025) *Viewing Generative AI and Children's Safety in the Round*. NSPCC Learning. Available at: https://learning.nspcc.org.uk/research-resources/2025/generative-ai-childrens-safety

National Youth Agency (NYA) (2024) *Youth Work Curriculum*. Available at: https://nya.org.uk/wp-content/uploads/2024/04/5.3.1-0923-NYA-Youth-Work-Curriculum-DIGITAL1-03.24-1.pdf

NHS (2022) *Symptoms of Post-Traumatic Stress Disorder (PTSD)*. Available at: www.nhs.uk/mental-health/conditions/post-traumatic-stress-disorder-ptsd/symptoms/

NHS (2023) *Fabricated or Induced Illness*. Available at: www.nhs.uk/mental-health/conditions/fabricated-or-induced-illness/overview/

Nolan, A. (2020) Poverty and children's rights. In J. Todres and S.M. King (eds), *The Oxford Handbook of Children's Rights*. Oxford: Oxford University Press.

Norman, R.E., Byambaa, M., De, R., Butchart, A., Scott, J. and Vos, T. (2012) The long-term health consequences of child physical abuse, emotional abuse, and neglect: a systematic review and meta-analysis. *PLOS Medicine*, 9(11). https://doi.org/10.1371/journal.pmed.1001349

Nunes, R.R. (2021) Participation in child protection: empowering children in placement processes. *International Journal of Human Rights*, 26(3), 420–36. https://doi.org/10.1080/13642987.2021.1931137

O Ciardha, C. and Ward, T. (2013) Theories of cognitive distortions in sexual offending: what the current research tells us. *Trauma, Violence and Abuse*, 14(1), 5–21. https://doi.org/10.1177/1524838012467856

O'Hagan, K. (1995) *Emotional and Psychological Abuse of Children*. London: Open University Press.

Ofcom (2024) *Risk Assessment Guidance and Risk Profiles*. Available at: www.ofcom.org.uk/siteassets/resources/documents/online-safety/information-for-industry/illegal-harms/risk-assessment-guidance-and-risk-profiles.pdf?v=390984

Office for Health Improvement and Disparities (OHID) (2022) *Working Definition of Trauma-Informed Practice*. Available at: www.gov.uk/government/publications/working-definition-of-trauma-informed-practice/working-definition-of-trauma-informed-practice

Office for National Statistics (ONS) (2019a) *Child Abuse Extent and Nature, England and Wales: Year Ending March 2019*. Available at: www.ons.gov.uk/peoplepopulationandcommunity/crimeandjustice/articles/childabuseextentandnatureenglandandwales/yearendingmarch2019

ONS (2019b) *Child Emotional Abuse in England and Wales: Year Ending March 2019*. Available at: www.ons.gov.uk/peoplepopulationandcommunity/crimeandjustice/articles/childemotionalabuseinenglandandwales/yearendingmarch2019?

ONS (2019c) *Child Sexual Abuse in England and Wales: Year Ending March 2019*. Available at: www.ons.gov.uk/peoplepopulationandcommunity/crimeandjustice/articles/childsexualabuseinenglandandwales/yearendingmarch2019"

ONS (2021) *Child Neglect in England and Wales*. Available at: www.ons.gov.uk/peoplepopulationandcommunity/crimeandjustice/articles/childneglectinenglandandwales/yearendingmarch2019

Office of the Children's Commissioner (OCC) (2012) *'I thought I was the only one. The only one in the world': The Office of the Children's Commissioner's Inquiry into Child Sexual Exploitation in Gangs and Groups*. Available at: www.childrenscommissioner.gov.uk/report/i-thought-i-was-the-only-one-in-the-world/

Online Safety Act 2023. Available at: www.legislation.gov.uk/ukpga/2023/50

Open University (n.d.) *Applying Social Work Law with Children and Families: 6.1 The Principle of Non-intervention*. Open Learn. Available at: www.open.edu/openlearn/society-politics-law/applying-social-work-law-children-and-families/content-section-6.1

Ortega, D. and Rodriguez-Jenkins, J. (2021) *Empowerment Practices*. Encyclopedia of Social Work. Available at: https://oxfordre.com/socialwork/view/10.1093/acrefore/9780199975839.001.0001/acrefore-9780199975839-e-128

Page, S., McFeeters, A., Mat Rani, N.H., Slater, C., Stevenson, J., Quayle, E. and Fry, D. (2025) Psychological and emotional harms of online child sexual exploitation and abuse in children under the age of 18: a systematic review of the evidence. *Child Abuse Review*. Advance online publication. https://doi.org/10.1002/car.70048

Parker, J. (2020) *Social Work Practice*. 6th edn. London: Sage.

Parker, J. and Ashencaen Crabtree, S. (2017) *Social Work with Disadvantaged and Marginalised People*. Exeter: Learning Matters.

Parton, N. (1998) Risk, advanced liberalism and child welfare: the need to rediscover uncertainty and ambiguity. *British Journal of Social Work*, 28, 5–27.

Parton, N. (2006) *Safeguarding Childhood*. Basingstoke: Palgrave Macmillan

Pears, K.C. and Capaldi, D.M. (2001) Intergenerational transmission of abuse: a two-generational prospective study of an at-risk sample. *Child Abuse and Neglect*, 25(11), 1439–61. https://doi.org/10.1016/S0145-2134(01)00286-1

Petersen, A.C., Joseph, J. and Feit, M. (eds) (2014) *New Directions in Child Abuse and Neglect Research: 4, Consequences of Child Abuse and Neglect*. Washington, DC: National Academies Press. Available from: www.ncbi.nlm.nih.gov/books/NBK195987/

Phillimore, S. (2020) How do children 'consent'? The interplay of 'Gillick competence' and 'parental responsibility'. *Childhood Protection Resource*. Available at: https://childprotectionresource.online/the-interplay-of-gillick-competence-and-parental-responsibility/#:~:text=Interplay%20between%20Gillick%20competence%20and,the%20exercise%20of%20parental%20responsibility

Porta, C.M., Frerich, E.A., Hoffman, S., Bauer, S., Jain, V.M. and Bradley, C. (2023) Sexual violence in virtual reality. *Journal of Forensic Nursing*, 20(1), 66–77. https://doi.org/10.1097/jfn.0000000000000466

Powell, F. and Scanlon, M. (2014) The media and child abuse. *Discover Society*, 13. https://archive.discoversociety.org/2014/09/30/the-media-and-child-abuse/

Prevention of Cruelty to, and Protection of, Children Act 1889. Available at: www.legislation.gov.uk/ukpga/Vict/52-53/44/contents/enacted

Protection of Children Act 1999. Available at: www.legislation.gov.uk/ukpga/1999/14

Public Services Committee Report (2025) Children in Crisis: The Role of Public Services in Supporting Vulnerable Children. Available at: https://committees.parliament.uk/publications/9261/documents/160274/default/

Pullen-Sansfaçon, A. and Cowden, S. (2012) *The Ethical Foundations of Social Work*. London: Routledge.

Radford, L., Corral, S., Bradley, C., Fisher, H., Bassett, C., Howat, N. and Collishaw, S. (2011) *Child Abuse and Neglect in the UK Today*. London: NSPCC.

Rafiq, H. and Adil, M. (2017) *Group-Based Child Sexual Exploitation: Dissecting 'Grooming Gangs'*. London: Quilliam.

Rakovski, C., Lalli, M., Gu, J., Hobson, M., Wollenhaupt-Aguiar, B., Minuzzi, L., Kapczinski, F., de Azevedo Cardoso, T. and Frey, B.N. (2024) Childhood maltreatment as a predictor of substance use/misuse among youth: a systematic review and meta-analysis. *Neuroscience and Biobehavioral Reviews* 66, 105873. https://doi.org/10.1016/j.neubiorev.2024.105873

Rayworth, B.B., Wise, L.A. and Harlow, B.L. (2004) Childhood abuse and risk of eating disorders in women. *Epidemiology* (Cambridge, MA), 15(3), 271–8. https://doi.org/10.1097/01.ede.0000120047.07140.9d

Report of the Care of Children Committee (1946) Available at: https://wellcomecollection.org/works/dvmncs2n

Report of the Historical Institutional Abuse Inquiry (2017) Available at: www.executiveoffice-ni.gov.uk/articles/historical-institutional-abuse-inquiry

Research in Practice (RIP) (2018) *Developing and Leading Trauma-Informed Practice: Leaders' Briefing*. Available at: https://tce.researchinpractice.org.uk/wp-content/uploads/2020/02/Developing-and-leading-trauma-informed-practice.pdf

Rogers, C.R. (1951) *Client-centred Therapy: Its Current Practice, Implications, and Theory*. Boston, MA: Houghton Mifflin.

Rowland, A., Gerry, F. and Stanton, M. (2017) Physical punishment of children: time to end the defence of reasonable chastisement in the UK, USA and Australia. *International Journal of Children's Rights*, 25(1), 165–95. https://doi.org/10.1163/15718182-02501007

Safeguarding Board for Northern Ireland (Membership, Procedure, Functions and Committee) Regulations (Northern Ireland) 2012. Available at: www.legislation.gov.uk/nisr/2012/324/contents/made

Safeguarding Network (2024) *Emotional Abuse*. Available at: https://safeguarding.network/content/safeguarding-resources/emotional-abuse/

Safeguarding Vulnerable Groups Act 2006. Available at: www.legislation.gov.uk/ukpga/2006/47/notes/division/2

Saleebey, D. (1996) The strengths perspective in social work practice: extensions and cautions. *Social Work*, 41(3), 296–305. www.jstor.org/stable/23718172

Saleebey, D. (2013) *The Strengths Perspective in Social Work Practice*. 6th edn. London: Pearson.

Salter, D., McMillan, D., Richards, M., Talbot, T., Hodges, J., Bentovim, A., Hastings, R., Stevenson, J. and Skuse, D. (2003) Development of sexually abusive behaviour in sexually victimised males: a longitudinal study. *The Lancet*, 361, 471–6. 10.1016/S0140-6736(03)12466-X

Sanders, R. and Mace, S. (2006) Agency policy and the participation of children and young people in the child protection process. *Child Abuse Review*, 15, 89–109. https://doi.org/10.1002/car.927

Sandford, D. (2024) Behind Sara's smile was a life of violence and torture. *BBC News*. Available at: www.bbc.com/news/articles/cvgedlr7qg1o

Saxena, M., Tote, S. and Sapkale, B. (2023) Multiple personality disorder or dissociative identity disorder: etiology, diagnosis, and management. *Cureus*, 15(11), e49057. https://doi.org/10.7759/cureus.49057

Schimmenti, A., Billieux, J., Santoro, G., Casale, S. and Vladan, S. (2022) A trauma model of substance use: elaboration and preliminary validation. *Addictive Behaviors*, 134, 107431. ISSN 0306-4603, https://doi.org/10.1016/j.addbeh.2022.107431

Scottish Child Abuse Inquiry (SCAI) (2024) *Scottish Child Abuse Inquiry Publishes Twelfth Case Study Findings*. Available at: www.childabuseinquiry.scot/news/scottish-child-abuse-inquiry-publishes-twelfth-case-study-findings

Scottish Government (2014) *National Guidance for Child Protection in Scotland 2014*. Edinburgh: Scottish Government.

Serious Crime Act 2015. Available at: www.legislation.gov.uk/ukpga/2015/9/contents

Sexual Offences Act 2003. Available at: www.legislation.gov.uk/ukpga/2003/42/contents

Seymour, A. (1998) Aetiology of the sexual abuse of children: an extended feminist perspective. *Women's Studies International Forum*, 21(4), 415–27. https://doi.org/10.1016/S0277-5395(96)00068-4

Shaw, I.F. (2021) Social work and sociology/sociology and social work: peering back and forth. *Qualitative Social Work*, 20(5), 1184–203. https://doi.org/10.1177/1473325020973300

Shaw, T. (2007) *Historical Abuse Systemic Review: Residential Schools and Children's Homes in Scotland 1950 to 1995*. Edinburgh: Scottish Government. Available at: www.scotland.gov.uk/Resource/Doc/203922/0054353.pdf

Skinner, A. (1992) *Another Kind of Home: Review of Residential Child care in Scotland*. Edinburgh: HMSO.

Sloth-Nielsen, J. (2008) Southern African perspectives on banning corporal punishment: a comparison of Namibia, Botswana, South Africa and Zimbabwe. In B. Saunders, P. Leviner and B. Naylor (eds), *Corporal Punishment of Children: Comparative Legal and Social Developments towards Prohibition and Beyond*. Leiden, Netherlands: Brill, pp. 245–66.

Smallbone, S., Marshall, W.L. and Wortley, R. (2008) *Preventing Child Sexual Abuse: Evidence, Policy and Practice*. Cullompton: Willan.

Smith, C.P. and Freyd, J.J. (2014) Institutional betrayal. *American Psychologist*, 69(6), 575–87. https://doi.org/10.1037/a0037564

Smith, M. and Monteux, S. (2023) *Trauma-informed Approaches: A Critical Overview of What They Offer Social Work and Social Care*. Available at: www.iriss.org.uk/resources/insights/trauma-informed-approaches-critical-overview-what-they-offer-social-work-and-social-care

Smith, R. (2008) *Social Work and Power*. Basingstoke: Palgrave Macmillan.

Smith, R. (2010) Social work, risk, power. *Sociological Research Online*, 15(1), 37–46. https://doi.org/10.5153/sro.2101

Social Care Institute for Excellence (SCIE) (2019) *Safeguarding Adults: Sharing Information*. Available at: www.scie.org.uk/safeguarding/adults/practice/sharing-information/

SCIE (2022) *Co-production: What It Is and How To Do It*. Available at: www.scie.org.uk/co-production/what-how/

Social Work England (SWE) (2019) *Professional Standards*. Available at: www.socialworkengland.org.uk/standards/professional-standards/

Springer, K.W., Sheridan, J., Kuo, D. and Carnes, M. (2007) Long-term physical and mental health consequences of childhood physical abuse: results from a large population-based sample of men and women. *Child Abuse and Neglect*, 31(5), 517–30. https://doi.org/10.1016/j.chiabu.2007.01.003

SWE (2025) *Supervision*. Available at: www.socialworkengland.org.uk/cpd/supervision/

Stainton-Rogers, W. (2001) Constructing childhood; constructing child concern. In P. Foley, J. Roche and S. Tucker (eds), *Children in Society: Contemporary Theory, Policy and Practice*. Basingstoke: Open University Press, pp. 26–33.

Stein, M. (2006) Missing years of abuse in children's homes. *Child and Family Social Work*, 11(1), 11–21. https://doi.org/10.1111/j.1365-2206.2006.00381.x

Stern, R.T. (2021) Incorporating the CRC in Sweden. In U. Kilkelly, L. Lundy and B. Byrne (eds), *Incorporating the UN Convention on the Rights of the Child into National Law*. Cambridge: Intersentia, pp. 205–30.

Stone, O.M. (1964) Children and Young Persons Act, 1963. *Modern Law Review*, 27(1), 61–70. www.jstor.org/stable/1092258

Substance Abuse and Mental Health Services Administration (SAMHSA) (2014) *SAMHSA's Concept of Trauma and Guidance for a Trauma-Informed Approach*. Available at: https://library.samhsa.gov/sites/default/files/sma14-4884.pdf

Sweeney, A. and Taggart, D. (2019) Embedding trauma-informed approaches in adult social care: frontline briefing. *Research in Practice for Adults*. Available at: www.researchinpractice.org.uk/media/hj0k0021/ripfa_embedding_trauma-informed_approaches_frontline_briefing_web.pdf Research in Practice

Sylvestre, A., Bussières, È.-L. and Bouchard, C. (2016) Language problems among abused and neglected children: a meta-analytic review. *Child Maltreatment*, 21(1), 47–58. https://doi.org/10.1177/1077559515616703

Tedeschi, R.G. and Calhoun, L.G. (1996) The posttraumatic growth inventory: measuring the positive legacy of trauma. *Journal of Traumatic Stress*, 9(3), 455–71. https://doi.org/10.1002/jts.2490090305

Tew, J. (2002) *Social Theory, Power and Practice*. Basingstoke: Palgrave Macmillan.

Tew, J. (2006) Understanding power and powerlessness: towards a framework for emancipatory practice in social work. *Journal of Social Work*, 6(1), 33–51. https://doi.org/10.1177/1468017306062222

The Survivors Trust (2025) *Survivor Stories*. Available at: https://thesurvivorstrust.org/survivor-stories/

Thompson, N. (2016) *Anti-discriminatory Practice: Equality, Diversity and Social Justice* (6th edn). Basingstoke: Palgrave Macmillan.

Thornberry, T.P., Knight, K.E. and Lovegrove, P.J. (2012) Does maltreatment beget maltreatment? A systematic review of the intergenerational literature. *Trauma, Violence and Abuse*, 13(3), 135–52. https://doi.org/10.1177/1524838012447697

Truth Project (2018) *Truth Project Experiences Shared: Victims and Survivors Speak Out*. Available at: https://webarchive.nationalarchives.gov.uk/ukgwa/20221214211449/www.iicsa.org.uk/key-documents/5462/view/truth-project-experiences-shared-june-2018.pdf

UK General Data Protection Regulation (GDPR). Available at: www.legislation.gov.uk/eur/2016/679/contents

UNDP (2023) Sustainable Development Goals: Progress Chart 2023. Available at: https://unstats.un.org/sdgs/report/2023/progress-chart/Progress-Chart-2023.pdf

Ungar, M. (2002) A deeper, more social ecological social work practice. *Social Service Review*, 76(3), 480–97. https://doi.org/10.1086/341185

UNICEF (1989) United Nations Convention on the Rights of the Child. Available at: www.unicef.org.uk/wp-content/uploads/2016/08/unicef-convention-rights-child-uncrc.pdf

UNICEF (2020a) *Mapping the Global Goals of Sustainable Development and the Convention on the Rights of the Child*. Available at: www.unicef.org/csr/css/UNICEF-SDG-CRC-Mapping.pdf

UNICEF (2020b) *Violence Against Children*. Available at: www.unicef.org/protection/violence-against-children

UNICEF (2024a) *Children's Version of the Convention on the Rights of the Child*. Available at: convention-rights-child-text-child-friendly-version.pdf

UNICEF (2024b) Frequently asked questions on the Convention on the Rights of the Child Available at: www.unicef.org/child-rights-convention/frequently-asked-questions

UNICEF (n.d.a) *Barnkonventionen*. Avaiilable at: https://unicef.se/barnkonventionen

UNICEF (n.d.b) *History of Child Rights*. Available at: www.unicef.org/child-rights-convention/history-child-rights

UNICEF and United Nations Population Fund (UNFPA) (2018) *Enabling Environments for Eliminating Female Genital Mutilation*. Available at: www.unicef.org/media/84536/file/FGM-Policy-Brief.pdf

UNICEF South Africa (2011) *South Africa's Children: A Review of Equity and Child Rights*. Available at: www.unicef.org/southafrica/media/1166/file/ZAF-south-africas-children-2011_1.pdf

United Nations (2015) *Transforming Our World: The 2030 Agenda for Sustainable Development*. Available at: https://sdgs.un.org/2030agenda

United Nations (2023) *Concluding Observations on the Combined 6th and 7th Periodic Reports of the United Kingdom of Great Britain and Northern Ireland*. Available at: https://digitallibrary.un.org/record/4013807?ln=en&v=pdf

United Nations General Assembly (UNGA) (1959) *Declaration of the Rights of the Child*. Available at: https://digitallibrary.un.org/record/195831/?v=pdf

United Nations Office on Drugs and Crime (UNODC) (n.d.) *Online Child Sexual Exploitation and Abuse*. Available at: https://sherloc.unodc.org/cld/en/education/tertiary/cybercrime/module-12/key-issues/online-child-sexual-exploitation-and-abuse.html

van Breda, A.D. (2022) Person-centred approaches to social work practice. In D. Hölscher, R. Hugman and D. McAuliffe (eds), *Social Work Theory and Ethics*. Singapore: Springer. https://doi.org/10.1007/978-981-16-3059-0_8-1

Vismara, M., Girone, N., Conti, D., Nicolini, G. and Dell'Osso, B. (2022) The current status of cyberbullying research: a short review of the literature. *Current Opinion in Behavioral Sciences*, 46, 101152. https://doi.org/10.1016/j.cobeha.2022.101152

Wade, T.J., Bowden, J. and Sites, H.J. (2017) Child maltreatment and motor coordination deficits among preschool children. *Journal of Child and Adolescent Trauma*, 11(2), 159–62. https://doi.org/10.1007/s40653-017-0186-4

Walker, K., Pillinger, C. and Brown, S. (2018) Characteristics and Motivations of Perpetrators of Child Sexual Exploitation. *Research Programme Report No. 2*. Available at: www.csacentre.org.uk/app/uploads/2023/10/CSE-perpetrators-2-Characteristics-and-motivations-of-perpetrators-of-CSE.pdf

Walklate, S. (2006) Changing boundaries of the 'victim' in restorative justice. In D. Sullivan and L. Tifft (eds), *Handbook of Restorative Justice*. Abingdon: Routledge, pp. 273–85.

Ward, H., Brown, R. and Maskell-Graham, D. (2012) *Young Children Suffering, or Likely to Suffer, Significant Harm: Experiences on Entering Education*. Research Report DFE-RR209. Available at: https://assets.publishing.service.gov.uk/government/uploads/system/uploads/attachment_data/file/184104/DFE-RR209.pdf

Weber, M. (1947) *The Theory of Social and Economic Organizations*. New York: Free Press.

Weidenstedt, L. (2016) Empowerment gone bad: communicative consequences of power transfers. *Socius: Sociological Research for a Dynamic World*, 2, 1–11. https://doi.org/10.1177/2378023116672869

Welsh Assembly Government (2008) *All Wales Child Protection Procedures 2008*. Available at: https://cysur.cymru/media/mrycc5qv/all_wales_child_protection_procedures_2008_1_.pdf

Whittier, N. (2009) *The Politics of Child Sexual Abuse: Emotion, Social Movements, and the State*. Oxford: Oxford University Press.

WHO (2022) *Violence Against Children*. Available at: www.who.int/news-room/fact-sheets/detail/violence-against-children

WHO (2025) *Female Genital Mutilation*. Available at: www.who.int/news-room/fact-sheets/detail/female-genital-mutilation

Widom, C.S. (1989) The cycle of violence. *Science*, 244(4901), 160–6. https://doi.org/10.1126/science.2704995

Widom, C.S., Czaja, S.J. and DuMont, K.A. (2015) Intergenerational transmission of child abuse and neglect: real or detection bias? *Science*, 347(6229), 1480–5. https://doi.org/10.1126/science.1259917

Wilkinson, J. and Bowyer, S. (2017) *The Impacts of Abuse and Neglect on Children; And Comparison of Different Placement Options: Evidence Review*. Available at: https://assets.publishing.service.gov.uk/government/uploads/system/uploads/attachment_data/file/602148/Childhood_neglect_and_abuse_comparing_placement_options.pdf

Williams, J.M. and Lee, E. (2024) A systematic review of cultural competence educational techniques in social work education. *International Social Work*, 68(3), 397–414. https://doi.org/10.1177/00208728241269769

Wilson, A. and Beresford, P. (2000) 'Anti-oppressive practice': emancipation or appropriation? *British Journal of Social Work*, 30(5), 553–73. https://doi.org/10.1093/bjsw/30.5.553

Winter, K. (2019) Relational social work. In M. Payne and E. Reith Hall (eds), *Routledge Handbook of Social Work Theory*. London: Routledge, pp. 1–10.

Wold, T., Aristodemou, E., Dunkels, E. and Laouris, Y. (2009) Inappropriate content. In S. Livingstone and L. Haddon (eds), *Kids Online: Opportunities and Risks for Children*. Bristol: Policy Press, pp. 135–46. https://doi.org/10.1332/policypress/9781847424396.003.0011

Wright, K. (2017) Remaking collective knowledge: an analysis of the complex and multiple effects of inquiries into historical institutional child abuse. *Child Abuse and Neglect*, 74, 10–22.

Xu, X., Tung, Y. and Dunaway, R.G. (2000) Cultural, human, and social capital as determinants of corporal punishment: toward an integrated theoretical model. *Journal of Interpersonal Violence*, 15, 603–30.

Zielinski, D.S. (2009) Child maltreatment and adult socioeconomic well-being. *Child Abuse and Neglect*, 33(10), 666–78. https://doi.org/10.1016/j.chiabu.2009.09.001

Index

FSC
www.fsc.org
MIX
Papier | Fördert gute Waldnutzung
FSC® C083411

Zeitfracht Medien GmbH
Ferdinand-Jühlke-Straße 7
99095 Erfurt, Deutschland
produktsicherheit@kolibri360.de